Red Light, Green Light

WALL STREET MONEY MACHINE

VOLUME 6

*"Our purpose in life should
be to build a life of purpose"*
—WADE B. COOK

Red Light, Green Light

WALL STREET MONEY MACHINE
VOLUME 6

WADE B. COOK

Lighthouse Publishing Group Inc.

Lighthouse Publishing Group, Inc.
Copyright © 2002 Never Ending Wealth, LP

Library of Congress Cataloging-in-Publication Data
Cook, Wade.
Wall street money machine, volume 6, red light, green light / Wade B. Cook
p. cm.
Includes bibliographical references and index.
ISBN 1-892008-68-8
1. Speculation. 2. Stocks. 3. Futures. I. Title.
HG6041.C64 1999
332.63'228-dc21   99-17010
                                                                    CIP

"This publication is designed to provide general information in regard to the subject matter covered. It is sold with the understanding that the publisher is not engaged in rendering legal, accounting, or other professional services. If legal, accounting, or other professional services are required, the services of an independent professional should be sought."

"From a declaration of principles jointly adopted by a committee of the American Bar Association and the committee of the Publisher's Association."

LEAPS® and Long-Term Equity AnticiPation Securities® are registered trademarks of the Chicago Board Options Exchange, Inc.

TC2000® and chart examples are copyright Worden Brothers.
Some charts are copright Bloomberg

Creative Director: Mark Engelbrecht
Book Design by Gina Lynd, Jennifer Stolz, Luke Keller, Mark Engelbrecht
Dust Jacket Design by Jennifer Stolz
Dust Jacket Photographs by Zachary Cherry
Inside Photograph by Vaughn Tanner

Published by Lighthouse Publishing Group, Inc.
14675 Interurban Avenue South
Seattle, Washington 98168-4664
1-800-706-8657   206-901-3027 (fax)

Source Code: WSMMV601

Printed in United States of America
10 9 8 7 6 5 4 3 2 1

To Carla, Diana, and
in loving memory of Benita,
my wonderful sisters,
who are masters of keeping
their family and friends
in life's exciting
green light periods.

BOOKS BY LIGHTHOUSE PUBLISHING GROUP, INC.

Two Bad Years and Up We Go! WADE B. COOK

THE WALL STREET MONEY MACHINE SERIES, WADE B. COOK
Wall Street Money Machine, Volume 1
Wall Street Money Machine, Volume 2: Stock Market Miracles
Wall Street Money Machine, Volume 3: Bulls & Bears
Wall Street Money Machine, Volume 4: Safety 1st Investing
Wall Street Money Machine, Volume 5: Free Stocks:
How to Get the Market to Pay for Your Stocks – FREE!

Stock Split Secrets: Profiting from a Powerful Predictable
Price-moving Event, DARLENE NELSON AND MILES NELSON
Beginning Investors Bible, DOUG SUTTON
On Track Investing, DAVID R. HEBERT
Rolling Stocks, GREGORY WITT
Sleeping Like A Baby, JOHN C. HUDELSON

Real Estate Money Machine, WADE B. COOK
101 Ways To Buy Real Estate Without Cash, WADE B. COOK
How To Pick Up Foreclosures, WADE B. COOK
Real Estate For Real People, WADE B. COOK

Blueprints For Success, WADE COOK AND VARIOUS OTHER AUTHORS
Brilliant Deductions, WADE B. COOK
Million Heirs, JOHN V. CHILDERS, JR.
The Secret Millionaire Guide To Nevada Corporations, JOHN V. CHILDERS, JR.
Wealth 101, WADE B. COOK

A+, WADE B. COOK
Business Buy The Bible, WADE B. COOK
Don't Set Goals (The Old Way), WADE B. COOK
Wade Cook's Power Quotes, Volume 1, WADE B. COOK
Success: American Style, WADE B. COOK

CONTENTS

PREFACE

It has been many years since I started teaching the Red Light, Green Light "newsy-go-round" style of trading. It has been a most remarkable time. The market was on a wild tear for many years, and then the Internet (dot-com) fever took over and propelled many dot-com stocks even higher, like rocket fuel. Into the stratosphere they went. Oxygen was scarce. These same stocks had a huge downturn when the fuel ran out.

Through all of this, I watched as my observations and subsequent trades were put to the test. I said several years ago that the Red Light, Green Light (RLGL) trading method would be one of the most significant discoveries of modern wealth building, especially if your purpose is to use the stock market to generate cash flow. Thousands upon thousands of people have benefited. Their trades are better – better entrance points, better exit points.

This book will explore the premise of creating more cash flow in the stock market. In a preface, let alone in a few paragraphs, it will be difficult to express the seriousness of the RLGL factor. Nevertheless, I will put a brief explanation here. As a CEO of a publicly traded company (Wade Cook Financial Corporation [OTCBB: WADE]), I noticed that stock and options prices rise and fall in regards to news reports and the anticipation of news reports. There are significant time periods each quarter when there is preparatory news from the company, then a quiet time followed by projections from outside news sources, actual filings, subsequent news reports and then a long quiet period when no news is dispensed. You can see this pattern played out repeatedly.

Stocks need news, and good news at that, to rise. Bad news and/or the lack of news is detrimental to the stock price. If you are playing options (which I suggest you not play until you understand them through study and practice trading [read *On Track Investing*, by Dave Hebert], then this news cycle will turn detrimental if you are not careful. You need to understand the importance of this question: "What compelling reason does this stock or option have to go up?" If there is no compelling reason for a stock to go up then it will probably go down. If you're playing stock options, the premium will be sucked out of the option value, time will deteriorate and you will lose. One purpose of writing this book is to help all of us to quit making mistakes. "Wishful Thinking" is not a valid trading method.

I keep using the word "trade," as opposed to "invest." Investing to me means giving up control. To "vest" means to own or have control over. We take our "vestments" and put them in someone else's control. If we invest in IBM, we as individuals do not control the operations of the company. We have little say about the direction of the company. We don't get to tell the board of directors how much of a dividend to pay. Our purchase or sale of 500 shares rarely impacts the market price of the stock. Now, however, if we trade the stock, say buy 500 shares at $92 on a major dip, and sell at $96 for a $4 profit, we're in control. If we sell the $90 put for $4 (ten contracts for $4,000) on the same dip and buy back the put for $2, profiting $2,000 when the stock rises to $96, that's trading. Trading is not investing; in fact, it's not even an investing style. It's completely different. Trading means getting our money in the way of movements and having a definite exit point. We buy so we can sell. We sell so we can buy back. We know our exit before we ever go in the entrance.

You can fight these movements, or you can learn them, track them, practice trade them, get to be an expert at a particular style and profit from them. We will not profit every time, but remember we just want to be right more than we are wrong. Understanding this RLGL phenomenon can truly stack the deck in our favor.

If you're just investing for the long term, this RLGL tracking device will have less of an impact on you. You'll want to visit Chapter 3 for insights on how to better your returns with your long-term investing method.

My seminars and books have had an impact on the way news media reports news about companies. For example, I was very critical of the way companies would revise their earnings forecast downward and then a few weeks later announce better earnings than the lowered estimates. You see, they had "built their forecasts." Now you hear remarks like this: "XYZ Company came in with earnings at 42¢ a share, 3¢ ahead of revised (or lowered) earnings forecasts." It takes guys like me to keep these people honest and not just pawns of the analysts. Having noted this, please understand my career is not to educate the major financial news sources, but to help my students, the "little guys," that no one else seems to care about.

There is one macro viewpoint I would like to make before you get on to learning how to trade better. Here it is: The stock market is an open air marketplace. Usually *current* stock prices reflect the anticipation of *future* earnings. Yes, there are other fundamental and technical viewpoints, but as I've said before – follow earnings, follow earnings, follow earnings.

Why do you think the Federal Reserve Board has taken such a primary role–literally center stage–in stock market movements? If they raise the discount rate a little, money will get tighter, harder to borrow, corporate earnings will fall in nine to twelve months, so the price goes down. Now, a year later, the Fed lowers rates, and the reverse happens–stock prices go up, because there is a projection of larger earnings in the future. Most movements are about earnings.

In the quarterly news cycle, this is exacerbated: The company beats projections, but then states (almost like lemmings into the sea) that future growth, or revenues, or earnings will slow down. The stock tanks. Lately, very few stocks have risen on great corporate news because of this incessant negative drumbeat. You can't fight market sentiment. You can learn and earn from it. It's almost as if you have to anticipate the anticipators.

I wish you well and pray for your prosperity.

Wade B. Cook

Wade B. Cook

ACKNOWLEDGMENTS

It takes a team to write a book like this. I am also sincerely grateful for the help of my many Team Wallstreet™ instructors who have not only taught our students well, but have shared many of their innovative and up-to-date ideas. The members of our Research and Training Department David McKinlay, Barry Collette, Jay Harris, and Paul Lund have given me extremely valuable help on a timely basis. Thanks also goes to Lighthouse Publishing Group, Jerry Miller who has been very helpful with this book, and to Jennifer Stolz, Mark Engelbrecht, and Luke Keller who put this book together. There have also been many other contributors to this effort. Also thanks to the Executive Staff at Wade Cook Financial Corporation, Robert Hondel, Cindy Britten, Robin Anderson, and Carol Taylor. They run the show so I can write. Also, heartfelt appreciation to my assistants Patsy Sanders and Cindy Little. And last, but not least, thanks goes to my wife, Laura. When God blessed me with Laura, He definitely upgraded me to First Class.

1

No News is Bad News

Lately, I've spent a lot of time in my seminars talking about and showing people how to increase their powers of observation and apply that to increasing their profits. For example, if you see patterns, say a connection between a company's stock dipping or rising at certain times as the stock goes through a split, can you not take advantage of this pattern? Can we not make better trades? Get in at more opportune times and get out with more cash?

The obvious is not always so obvious. I demonstrate this in classes by getting everyone to sing *Twinkle, Twinkle, Little Star* as a group while I sing *Now I Know My ABCs*. These songs have the same melody, as does *Baa Baa Black Sheep*. The point is that these are two of the songs most widely sung by American children, who learned them from their parents, and rarely does anyone realize they are the same melody.

We need to get better at connecting the dots. I look for connections in the stock market all the time and then try to figure out how to capitalize on those observations. I've recently discovered something so pervasive, so recognizable, that once you know and "get it," it will literally shake up a lot of things you do. It will help you avoid mistakes. It will help you trade better – better execution and more cash profits.

What I am about to explain is a price movement phenomenon based on the market's reaction to events on the corporate calendar. Many people have observed parts of this phenomenon. Others see one angle of it but don't see the connection. Still others see the same patterns and time periods but don't understand the "why" behind the stock movements. If you don't truly understand this cause and effect, it's hard to build faith in it – to formulate your "law" and put that law to work for you.

Your stockbroker or financial planner may claim to have known about this concept. If so, chew that person out for not telling you. Anyway, I doubt they know the entirety of this process. I've not talked to one person yet who understood all of this before I explained it – no broker, surely no news writer or journalist, and no other author.

You are about to read probably the single most important thing about trading in the stock market you have ever read or will ever read. I call it "Red Light, Green Light." This pearl of business wisdom was found through years of struggle, and you minimalize this process at your trading peril. Watch and be wise.

CHRONOLOGICAL CONNECTIONS

In May of 1995 I took our company public. Our assets grew rapidly and we became a reporting company June 30, 1996, when the quarterly SEC reports are filed. The June 30 reports actually had to be filed within 45 days, or by August 15. This important point will come back into play later. Read on.

For years now my accounting and legal departments have worked on our quarterly and annual reports. During this quarterly process, there are windows which open or close on what I, as a CEO, Board member and insider can say. There are also specific time periods when I can and cannot sell my own company's stock.

I can pretty much *buy* stock whenever. It's in the selling of that stock or other stock holdings where restrictions exist. If I buy stock in a company wherein I am considered an insider (a person with information that the general public does not have access to), then I have to hold onto the stock for six months. If I do sell it before six months are up, say to recover my cash, I will have to give back to the company any profits I've made. This is called disgorgement. I'm not allowed to make a profit on the stock based on "inside" information. These rules are good. They protect the investing public.

After years of complying and being careful when to buy and sell (actually as of this writing I've never sold any stock in WCFC; I want to own more of it), and being careful of what I say when, I started observing things. Here it is plain and simple: News drives stock prices. Everyone knows this. But it is only one component, one piece of the puzzle.

Here's the question I asked myself. If I, as a CEO, am under all these restrictions – these open and closed window periods of time – then what about the 25,000 or so other CEOs, CFOs, COOs, CLOs, Boards of Directors and other insiders of all publicly traded companies in this wonderful country? Are they not under the same requirements?

Also, there are restrictions on what we can do with the stock. We have windows of opportunity when we can buy the stock and we also have windows when we can sell the stock. Now pretty much across the board, except right before earnings, anybody as an insider can buy stock in a company, but they cannot sell the stock for six months and make a profit on it. If they do make a profit, they'd have to do what's called disgorgement; they would have to disgorge the profits back to the company. So for example they bought a stock at $18 and the stock went up to $22, they have every right to recover their $18 in less than six months, but if the stock is sold at $22 they'd have to return that extra $4 to the company. This is the way it should be.

Important Dates

This is where the next piece of the puzzle falls into place. When can "insiders" talk? When do they have to go silent? And what effect does this quarterly phenomenon have on the rise and fall of their stock prices? We'll explain all of these as we move along, but first some important dates.

December 31	This is the year end for most companies. SEC filings must be submitted for the whole year, and this document must be audited by an outside firm. The filing deadline is 90 days later, or March 31.
March 31 June 30 September 30	These are calendar quarter ends. Quarterly SEC filings may be unaudited. Filings are due 45 days later, on May 15, August 15 and November 15. Do you see an overlapping time period in the March 31 area? December 31 filings for the previous year need to be made as a company is just finishing up its first quarter.

Another point: some companies may use months other than December as their year end. Most companies have a December 31 year end, but even if they don't, they usually choose a calendar quarter to be their year end. Why? The answer lies in this quick but powerful observation: Companies must file their 940s and 941s (and other Federal and State filing requirements). Now if you've been in business you've already thought, "Aha, I got it!" But some of you have never had to do quarterly employment filings. Our benevolent government makes everyone file at the same time – in this case on a calendar quarter. If you chose a different year end other than a calendar quarter, it will seem as if you have to have two sets of records – one for yourself and one for the government. Hence, for ease of paperwork most companies comply and have their year end on one of the four calendar quarters. This one fact alone will have dynamic effects as a vast majority of companies fall in line and march together, doing the same thing at the same time. You'll see the dramatic effects of this process as you learn more about "red light, green light" news periods. There are timely things that have to be done and within those time periods, as each calendar quarter marches on, there are times when different kinds of news are given out to the general public.

So, to summarize, not all companies have the same calendar year end (December 31st), but almost all companies have the same calendar quarter ends. Some don't, like Dell. The patterns that follow quarterly reporting are somewhat predictable depending on the quality of the news. We'll get to that very soon.

News — Changing Perceptions

Now let's talk about news. For this discussion there are two types of news. There is internal news from the company: a company coming out with earnings reports or actual earnings, the earnings statements, share buybacks, mergers, acquisitions of other companies, changes of the Board of Directors and things like that. There's also news written by outside people like journalists and other analysts. They write reports about a company. This is external news. It's all important. As we go through this play I'm going to show you how this all works together.

Okay, let's start down the path. It's about June 15 – a few weeks before the quarter ends. People start to talk. Analysts adjust and re-adjust their expected earnings numbers. The CEO of a big company comes out in interviews or news releases and downplays the numbers, saying something like, "Sales have been good, but we have a charge off, so earnings will be $1.12 instead of $1.32." The stock drops $5, from $86 to $81. Now towards the end of June other news – mergers, share buybacks, takeovers, stock splits, other sales figures, new product announcements, *et cetera* – hits the streets. The stock wavers but heads back up.

Of all these newsy items, the type of announcement most followed is any announcement having to do with earnings (see *Wall Street Money Machine, Volume 2: Stock Market Miracles*). I've written about earnings, or P/E, in many other places. Many people base what they are willing to pay for a stock on the P/E, or price-to-earnings ratio. A typical NYSE company has a P/E of around 20 – let's say 19.2. In short, this means that the stock will cost $19.20 for every $1.00 of earnings. The stock may be at $250 or $5 or 50¢, it matters not. Now a static or isolated P/E is not the only factor in price determination even for those who only follow P/Es. Other important considerations include these questions: Are earnings growing or contracting? How does this company's earnings compare to those of other companies? Are earnings even a viable measurement in certain sectors? Internet stocks are a scary diversion from sound, rational practice in stock choices. Many have no "E" in their P/E.

Back to the point: Earnings is the most widely watched measurement of stock values. Because of this, all CEOs must be very careful of what they say about earnings.

Let's move down to the first week of July. The quarter is over, but the actual filing (10Q) has not yet been done. That will happen in a few weeks–at least by August 15, the filing deadline. Now, think this through. If the CEO, CFO or other corporate bigwigs comment about actual numbers before the proper documents are filed, it is assumed that he or she knows what the numbers should be. Do you see? Even if the accountants aren't through with the complete consolidated numbers, it would be determined that he or she should know. Because of this there is a complete news shutdown. No one will talk until the 10Qs are filed and the news release is out. Funny thing – the stock gets back to $86 and even up to $88. How does this happen? There is something happening here. Paranoia strikes deep. It is as if a whole group of people know something we don't know. In fact, we're the last to know.

Here's the pathetic, yet comical irony. Now the news is out – it's official. The interviews or press releases start up with something like this: "Earnings are ahead of expectations by about 10%. They are $1.22 per share." As the report goes on, you'll see an interesting twist. "We're pleased with the numbers and growth, but we contemplate a slowdown in sales next quarter (or year) and may not be able to maintain these high numbers."

Is this crazy or what? They good-mouth and bad-mouth their numbers in the same breath. Why? You must understand the fear these CEOs and others live under. They do not want to be seen as hyping their stock. They couch the truth behind caveats. They pad everything. This is the way it is.

Now another unusual thing happens. Many times the stock goes down in spite of good news. It is a strange phenomenon. I'm still perplexed when this happens. It's part of the "buy on rumors, sell on facts (news)" syndrome. Sometimes it has to do with what has happened to the stock in the few weeks or months before the report. It has a lot to do with sentiment – expectations and the like. There are too many variables to mention in this chapter. It's a mystery wrapped in a conundrum engulfed in an enigma.

Based on many other news developments, so goes the stock. One event is particularly important: the Board of Directors meeting. The date of this event can be checked out, and nothing happens until they meet. This is significant. They discuss profits, available cash for dividends, mergers, share buy backs, stock splits, business plans, et cetera.

Do you see how important these topics are? Think of all the guesswork going on by people following the company. Rumor fires are easily kindled. Sometimes they get out of control. However they start, whatever they are, it all ends when the actual numbers and news hit the street.

All of this is very important, but then what? Where's the sequel? Where's the new news? It's now the end of July or first week of August. (The same could be applied to the end of the October/November or January/February or April/May periods.) The news is out. We don't have to wait as long as we did for *Episode I: The Phantom Menace* to come out in the *Star Wars* series, but wait we must. In short, in the absence of news, "this stock ain't going nowhere." The balloon isn't going up without hot air. The car isn't leaving the garage without gas. Superman isn't flying without his cape.

Here's a problem. What if we purchase stock at the height of this incredible (pre) news time? The stock has risen to $92. A big firm puts out a buy rating. Others follow. The company even announces a stock split for August 20, a Friday. It just looks peachy – how can you lose?

Oh, and what if you like options? Those funny little derivatives which rise and fall as the stock does – and erode as the time moves on toward the expiration date.

Options present an awesome opportunity to make money as long as the stock moves exactly like you want it to. If you buy a call option–the right to buy stock–you want the stock to go up. If it goes down or stays the same, you lose. Now ask yourself: why am I buying this option when all the news has played out? At least ask, why did I buy the option with a near term expiration date? Maybe I should have bought the option with an expiration date at least into the next news reporting period.

Now all in all, observing this "news-no news" period should help us make wiser decisions. Decisions when to get in, decisions when to sell. Here is an important question: "What compelling reason does this stock have to go up?" More importantly, what compelling reason does this option have to go up in value? The answer is simple, but far-reaching. If there is nothing to drive it up – no news, no rumors, no nothing – then watch out.

Do you see where I now come up with *Red Light, Green Light*? A time to buy; a time *not* to buy. Now, notice I didn't say a time to sell. There are times when we should not be buying options. This goes back to a premise I've taught for years: the way to win at the stock market is to not lose! We need to avoid making mistakes. Buying a call option when a stock has nothing going on to help drive up the price is likely to be one of those mistakes.

A LOOK AT THE CALENDAR

By now you should have picked up on the important quarterly news periods. It helps sometimes to lay out a timeline or picture of the process. Before I do so, let's look again at a few things.

1. There are no set dates on which all companies start announcing newsy things. The dates vary. They are different because the Board may meet at odd times. After the Board meets the company may still make no announcement for several days or even weeks.

2. Many companies make very few pre-announcements, if any at all. Some make a lot. These announcements start about two weeks before the quarter end. Often you'll hear, "Well, we're entering the earnings season," meaning that news is about to come out. Some people "get it" on this part of the whole process. What you'll never hear from TV and newspaper reporters is this: "Well, we're leaving the earnings reporting season." Before I go on to number three, let me tell an interesting story:

We were having our speaker training two-day session in March, actually the Ides of March (March 15) and the day after. It was in Seattle. We were discussing Microsoft. It's on everyone's mind in Seattle, as it's a Northwest company. There are news reports on Microsoft almost daily in our region.

The stock had been floundering from the middle of February through that time. I was explaining this whole new "news-no news" concept to our instructors. After awhile, the subject of Microsoft came up. It was about 9 or 10 am on Monday. I pointed out that the stock was down and had been stagnant for a few weeks. I said, "Microsoft needs March 15. Oh, it is March 15th! So the news announcements should start soon."

Shortly, news came out over the wire about the company laying a foundation to break up into five divisions in anticipation of a lawsuit settlement with the Feds. The stock went up a couple of dollars. A little while later there was more news. This time they announced that they might enter an agreement, or that they were in talks to possibly end the lawsuit. Up another dollar or so.

The next morning, March 16th, the word on the street was that they were going to blow away their numbers – meaning they were making more money than expected. All in all the stock was up something like $7 to $8 in those two days. I looked at my great instructors and said, "Seeeeeeeeeee?"

It doesn't take a genius to figure out that if there's bad news, especially about earnings, or no news, that the stock will go down. Anticipation and expectation of news reports play a big part of this game. If there's good news or rumors of good news, the stock reacts accordingly. The old expression, "no news is good news" is out the window here. It's the opposite now: "No news is bad news" is more like it.

This leads up to number 3.

3.   A lot of stock movement depends on the quality of the news. At the time of this writing our economy is doing well. Many companies are earning a lot of money. A few are struggling. My guess

is that 20% of today's news is bad and about 80% is good. This will change.

So with a lot of good news hitting the streets, why do some stocks go down? One answer is that many investors think they can't keep up this level of profits. Dell, for example, went up (had positive earnings announcements) 32 quarters in a row. One quarter – the winter of 99 – they just hit their earnings estimates and the stock tanked. They're still a great company, earning millions, but some anticipate future sluggishness and the stock reacts. The marketplace is a giant auction. A stock goes for what someone will pay for it. Built into this are many factors, and one of the most important is anticipation of future earnings growth.

Check the quality of the news. Watch for news on one company and how it affects others in the same field. Observing this will let you see many buying and selling opportunities.

4. Not all companies follow the same exact time schedule. Many space out their announcements over a few days. Many make all of the news announcements at one time.

Often these announcements are known "on the street" way before the press conference. Ask your broker about the "whisper numbers." See what other companies have done. Try to get a handle on the direction of the stock. Most importantly, be careful of buying call options or stocks going into or in the middle of a "red light" no news period. Look for compelling reasons for a stock to increase. If you find none, watch out. Back off. Consider selling your calls or stocks in the midst of the newsy "green light" period—wait through the "red light" period, and buy again on dips on the other side of the red light time when the new news starts up again.

If the news is negative or the "red light" period has started, consider buying puts or doing Bear Call Spreads (see *Wall Street Money Machine, Volume 4: Safety 1st Investing*). In short, time your entrance and exit points for later.

Read the following information on a 1999 Microsoft announcement. See the nature of the news. See the "good mouthing" and "bad mouthing" that goes on.

MICROSOFT ANNOUNCES REORGANIZATION

REDMOND, Wash. – March 29, 1999 – Microsoft President Steve Ballmer and CEO Bill Gates today announced a sweeping reorganization, designed to refocus the company on the needs of customers.

The heart of the restructuring is the creation of distinct customer-centered business groups:

- The Business and Enterprise Division, which will focus on the information technology needs of large organizations.
- The Consumer Windows Division, which will focus on improving Windows for the end user.
- The Business Productivity Group, which will focus on the needs of the "knowledge worker" who is on the road and always in need of his or her data.
- The Developer Group, which will focus on helping developers who write software for all Microsoft platforms,
- The Consumer and Commerce Group, which will work to make it easier for customer and businesses to get together online.

The business divisions will think and act in parallel, each driving product planning and marketing strategies for customers. The customer-focused parallelism represents a move away from the alignment by products and technologies that Microsoft has used since its founding.

"This new structure is part of the reinvention of Microsoft," said Ballmer.

Another part of that reinvention is a broadened new vision.

"Our original vision of 'a computer on every desk and in every home' is still extremely relevant," said Gates. "Looking to the future our vision is much more expansive. We see a world where people can use any computing device to do whatever they want to do anytime, anywhere. The PC will continue to have a central role in this future, but it will be joined by an incredibly rich variety of digital devices accessing the power of the Internet."

"We want to give people the power, connectivity and the ability to choose how they want to use computing in their lives," Gates added.

Ballmer also announced the formation of a new Business Leadership Team. This team will replace the Executive Committee formed in December 1996, as the most senior-level decision-making team at the company. Members of the team will include: Jim Allchin, Orlando Ayala, Steve Ballmer, Brad Chase, Jon DeVaan, Bill Gates, Bob Herbold, Laura Jennings, Joachim Kempin, Greg Maffei, Paul Maritz, Mich Mathews, Bob Muglia, Bill Neukom and Jeff Raikes.

THE YEAR – UPS AND DOWNS

Look at the following 14-month graph. Note, this is a generality. *Any particular* stock's movement is based on many things – certainly not just a chart.

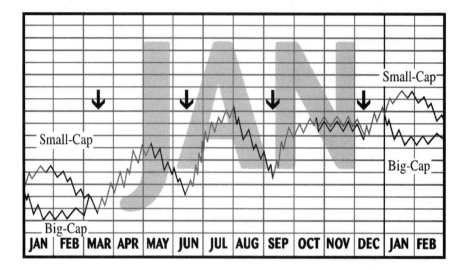

Observe:

1. The serious dips are in February, May, August, a neutral November and bad first two weeks of December.

2. October is a strange month with many erratic movements.

3. Look at the arrows. These represent the start of the news talk, the "green light" period.

4. The months following the year end are erratic because of the quality of the news, plus share buybacks and stock splits.

   Imagine now with me the following:

1. A company's stock goes up $10 in March. In late February or early March they announced a two-for-one stock split. The stock is splitting in the middle of May–a "red light" or no news period.

Look again at May on the Red Light, Green Light chart. Many stocks tank. Also note this is 2001. The whole market was dismal. How tough is it to make money in May, especially with short term options? There is a compelling reason to get out of the way (or buy Puts).

Explore the following charts. Remember, Red Light or Green Light does not mean good or bad. It means news and no news, and the news can be bad, as much of it was, in 1999 and 2001.

QUALCOMM

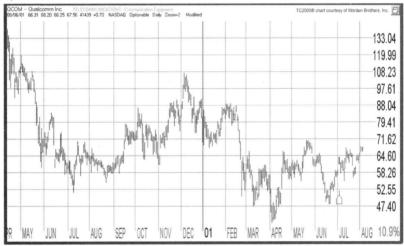

IBM

2. Look at the following charts for MSFT, INTL, and DELL. When
    a high tech stock has good news, several more rise up with it.
    But look at the subsequent month or so. They all move <u>up</u> or
    <u>down</u> based on news or no news.

MICROSOFT

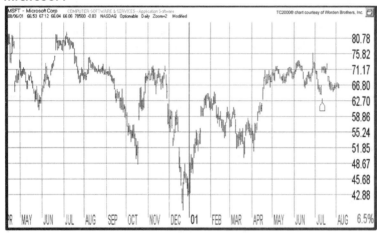

Again, May = no news. News in June through July. August, watch
out through most of September. October is erratic. November is flat.
After the first week (few days) of December many stocks go down
and then the news starts (pre-year end) and many stocks rally into
the year end and January.

INTEL

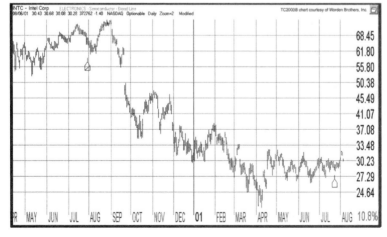

DELL

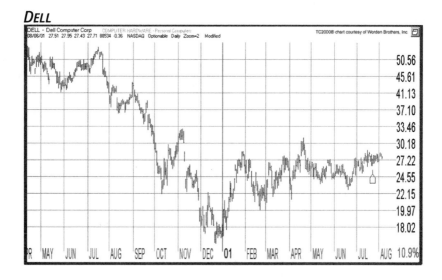

Note the January's. I've just written a Special Report on the top ten reasons for the January effect, or the January bounce. Call 1-800-872-7411 to order it.

A FEW OF THE DOW 30

Here are some Dow 30 stocks. Even if the stock is on an uptrend or a downtrend, the good (news) months and bad (no news) months are pronounced. Remember irregularities are caused by the quality of the news and other factors, i.e. announcements. Be careful when you buy options which expire in red light months. The big gaps in the stock line usually represent a stock split.

I'm going to include five more Dow 30 stocks here so you can see how they fit the pattern. I'll comment more in another chapter where we look at exceptions, pattern breakers and how to use my thirteen cash flow strategies in light of the *Red Light, Green Light* process.

CITIGROUP

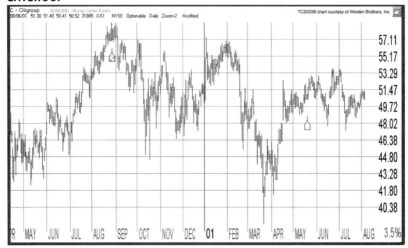

Maybe February would be a good month for a vacation. At least, get your money out of harms way.

GENERAL ELECTRIC

It seems this one is a week or so off kilter. It's a big company and there's plenty of news–almost constantly.

AT&T

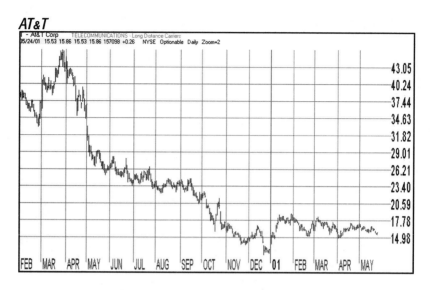

Look at February and May of both years.

AOL TIME WARNER

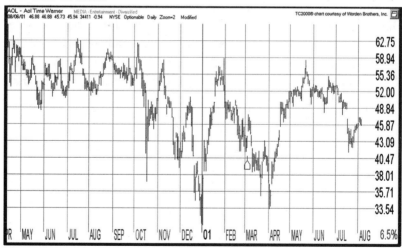

MERCK & CO

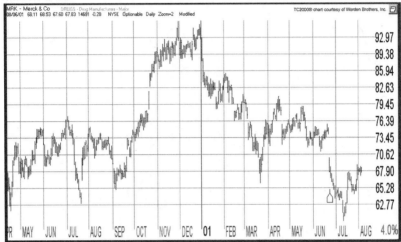

SUMMARY

This chapter has been about making better decisions, timing our entrance and exit points for more enhanced cash flow. The more dots we connect, the better for this process, the better for our bottom line. We also discussed the quantity of news–how even the company's "anticipation of news" period drives a stock up or down. Option trades need movement in the right direction to be profitable. Before buying calls or puts, ask the all-important question: What compelling reason does the stock have to go up (or down for puts)? If you don't have a good answer, then refraining from trading may be the best trade.

2

Making Better Trades

This chapter will give additional information and insights into my *Red Light, Green Light* process. All of this is to help you do more and better trades. This business aspect of the stock market is so different that it is no wonder most critics don't get it. It's easy to buy stocks or options, but difficult to close out a trade and make actual cash profits. If I were teaching people how to run a carpet cleaning business or a gas station, "buy wholesale, sell retail" would make sense, but in the market, people have a tough time selling or ending positions.

"Treat the stock market like a business" is now being understood by countless thousands. Here's an insight worth observing and then applying to the market: virtually every business has busy times or peak periods, such as summer travel, Christmas shopping, April 15th tax deadlines, *et cetera*. The *Red Light, Green Light* system is the same. There are four busy times a year and four not-so-busy or bad times a year. Granted you don't shut down your store in February because Christmas is over, but you also watch your inventory, your advertising costs and your payroll.

If you know that March/April, then June/July, September/October and lastly November and the second half of January are your busy times, then load up for those times.

If you need to make $X to live on, then do more trades during times with the highest probability of success. "Make hay while the sun shines." Why play calls in 'no news' periods and fight the trend – short-term though it is? Also, why just do a few trades? $10,000 could become $20,000 with 5 to 7 well placed $2,000 trades. Decisions need to be timely as well as quick.

HISTORY – DOES IT REPEAT?

I've never been one for believing that history always repeats itself. It does only if we don't study it and figure out ways to avoid the same stupid mistakes.

Looking for patterns on a quarterly basis caused me to question many people. One stockbroker faxed me the graphs on the following pages. These graphs cover a period of 40+ years. At first and even second glance they really get my head twirling. They proved so much of my own studies – and so much of my intuition.

What I don't know about these graphs is what components they used, and what controls existed for the study. I also know that this study ended in 1991. I'm almost confident that the same things happened on a quarterly basis, year in and year out.

At the end of section I'll put in the charts for 1991 through this time of 2000. But first let's deal with the 90s. I'm sure most of us had never heard of the Internet before 1991. I also realize that computer usage is and has been on the upswing for years. We were in an incredible bull market but I know also that much of the growth – the high performance – has been from a relatively small number of stocks.

The Internet is changing much of our way of life – shopping, research, genealogy and even financial seminars are changing. Many companies that didn't even exist five years ago are trading at billions of dollars in capitalization. It's breathtaking. The spread and easy access to doing transactions is welcomed by most people and will make many Americans and others very, very rich.

I also know the pioneers are not always the ultimate winners. Companies yet unborn will be the high-tech conglomerates of tomorrow.

Still, though, I think that *how* people file securities and other financial information is not as important as *when* they file it and the market's anticipation and reaction to this type of news. Finally, companies are making money on the Internet. Ironically, some of these startups have had their stocks climb to Mount Everest heights. Also ironically, it could be on actual earnings reports, when investors realize increasing or sustained earnings are limited, that these stocks may back off. Look for companies with real cash flow potential.

THE 50S, 60S, 70S AND 80S

These are my wonder years and it gets more wonderful all the time. Look at my remarks once again as to what stocks do throughout the year, primarily based on news filings in conjunction with or addition to the companies' SEC reporting requirements.

Now look at 40 years of S&P research on a monthly graph.

MARKET PERFORMANCE EACH MONTH OF THE YEAR
40 1/3 Years (January 1950-April 1991)

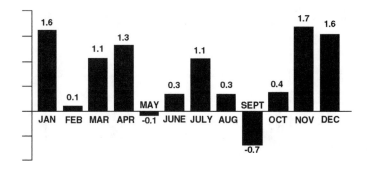

Look hard at this graph. Remember, these are historical averages for the market in general. A particular stock may move its own way. (If you do not see the "opportunity" times and the "caution" times then go back and start over.) Do not pass Go. Do not collect $200.

MOVING ON

Now let's look at a 40 year breakdown by the days of the month. Do you still see trends? Please don't think that because a particular day is bad historically, that it will be so this year. Yes, this year is different. Every year is different. It takes high days and low days to get an average. Averages don't tell you exactly what September 14, 2002 will do. All this information is good to add to our knowledge base so we have many (hopefully) contrasting opinions upon which we base our decision.

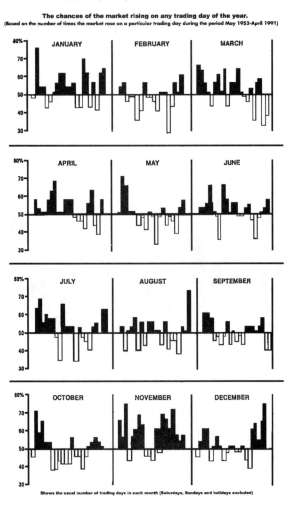

MARKET PROBABILITY CHART

The chances of the market rising on any trading day of the year.
(Based on the number of times the market rose on a particular trading day during the period May 1952-April 1991)

Shows the usual number of trading days in each month (Saturdays, Sundays and holidays excluded)

Let's look at more Dow stocks. We have gone through an incredible bull market, with the last two years showing a major correction. Some companies are still trying to find themselves as they fight negative news in a particular sector or in the marketplace in general.

Here is my brief statement about the movements of stock prices in and out of Red Light, Green Light periods. Remember, the real significance of these news periods is just that–news is anticipated, news is out, news is commented on and then news ends. Overriding this is the positive or negative characteristic of the particular event. For example, you might think green light means go. No, green light means the news goes, but it could be bad news and prices go down. You might check the quality, the length and the fine print of each news event. Also, a company is not bound by these dates. Right in the middle of a no-news period, a company could announce a major price moving event.

The year. January is usually an up month with a lot of new money coming into the market. February is a downer until about the middle of March and it picks up through April. May usually stinks until about the middle of June. It picks up through July and gets weak in August. (Note: August of 2000 was good). Again, with news turning off the second part of August and into September it gets weak again. October picks up, but October has an erratic nature to it. November usually holds its own, then December. Ah, December. Quite often the market backs off up to the middle of December and then there is often a rally into the end of the year. Then back to January.

3M

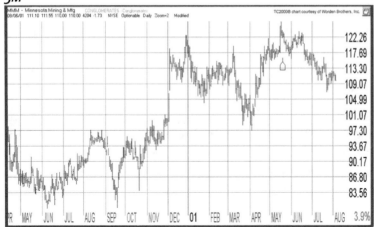

WAL-MART

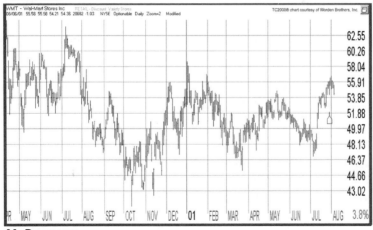

MCDONALDS

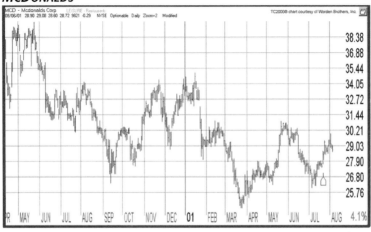

KODAK

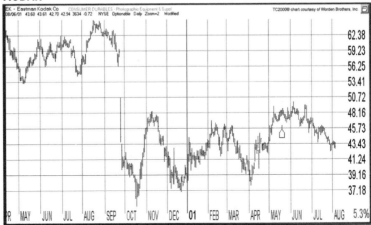

JOHNSON & JOHNSON

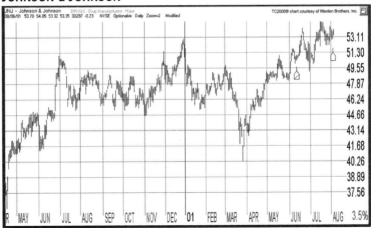

COCA-COLA

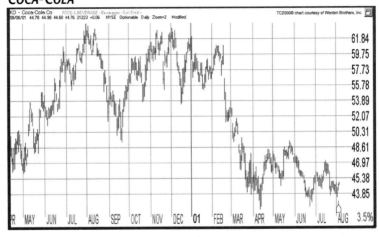

CATERPILLAR

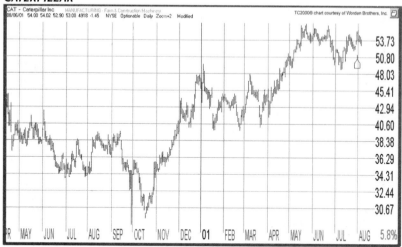

DUPONT

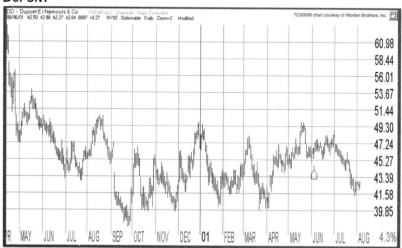

Boeing

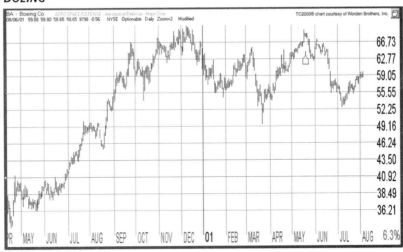

Honeywell

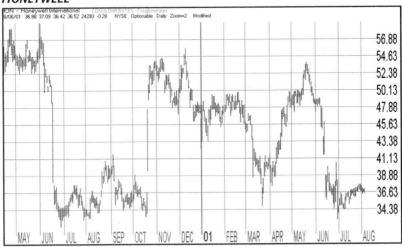

Now let's look at four high-flying Internet stocks. They moved up and down in the late 90s, but look at the pullbacks – can you spell BUYING OPPORTUNITY?

AOL TIME WARNER

CMGI

Yahoo!

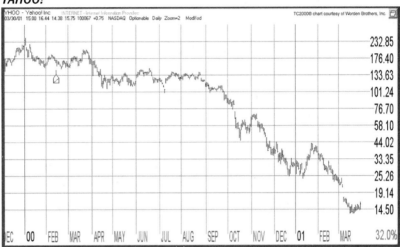

Amazon.com

As promised, let's now look at complete-year charts for the past several years. This will pick up where the previous S&P study left off.

The previous 40 year historical charts (page 35 & 36) ended in 1991. Here are the charts of the bigger market for every year through 2001. We've used the Standard & Poors 500. We ended this before the September 11th Terrorist attack as that event skewed everything.

There are several important things to notice.

1) December pull back and year end rally. This is important if you're playing December options, which expire on the third Friday of December.

2) The years 1998 and 1999 show a great bull market, but often, even in a rise, the stocks move up and down through their respective news, no news periods.

3) 2000 and 2001 show an inevitable down time. Still, look at the quarterly movements.

4) Remember, not all stocks are on a calendar quarter. Dell for example, in may 2001, came out with good news, and the whole market went up about 400 points in one day, with more the next few days. Talk about news–or even the anticipation of good news–driving the market, this shows it.

S&P 500, 1991

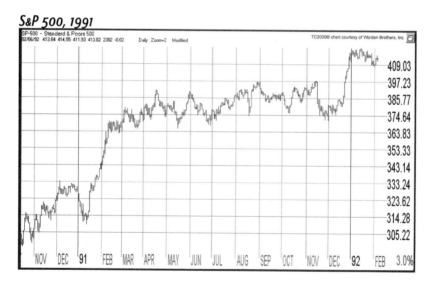

S&P 500, 1992

S&P 500, 1993

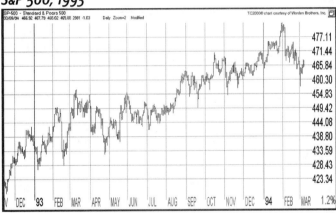

S&P 500, 1994

S&P 500, 1995

S&P 500, 1996

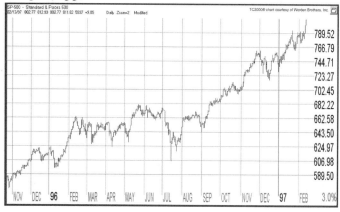

S&P 500, 1997

S&P 500, 1998

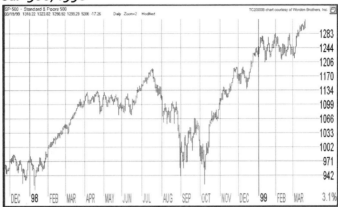

S&P 500, 1999

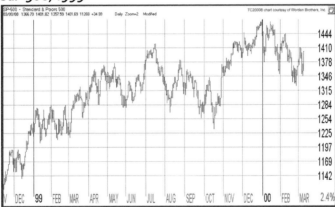

S&P 500, 2000

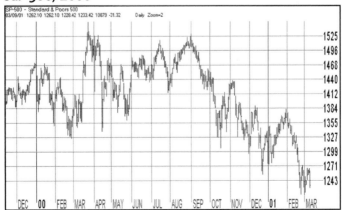

1999 saw a nice uptrending market but the trend did not hold through 2000.

One way to use this information is to get a chart of any company you're thinking of buying, stock or options, and line them up. Remember the question: What compelling reason does it have to go up?

Also this should help you choose better exit points. The trades work or not. If it works, great! Take the profit and run. If it doesn't work, get out of the canoe before it goes over the waterfall.

3

ITS ALL ABOUT ATTITUDE

"Develop the hunter's attitude, the outlook that wherever you go, there are ideas waiting to be discovered."
— ROGER VON OECH

Y ou bring with you into every situation the culmination of your experiences (good or bad), your opinions (whether they're on target or off target); your dreams (both active and dormant); your attempts (both successes and failures) and your prejudices (both helpful and hurtful). For me to convince you to do anything is a major accomplishment. To say the least, it's an uphill struggle.

However, I have hundreds of thousands of people who have benefited greatly because I refuse to give up on them. I am who I am and I want to be the very best, the number one financial educator in the country. To many, I've made it, but maybe not to you.

The following is an excerpt from my book, *A+*:

GREAT THINGS DON'T HAPPEN BY COMMITTEE

I am going to review an experience I have spoken about in almost every seminar and have written in almost every one of my books. It is so important to me. It is about seeking guidance.

Remember, even great Abraham went to pay tithes to Melchizedek the priest? Christ sent the healed persons to the priests. Why? I think the answer is found in a marvelous conversation Jesus had with Peter. He told Peter to "feed my sheep" and to strengthen the brethren. Jesus didn't tell Peter to do so whenever Peter felt like it, but when he was converted.

I see a lot of problems, both financially and spiritually, when people seek help from the wrong people. One question I ask in my seminars is, "How many of you want to make over $100,000 a year?" Almost all of the hands go up. Then I ask, "If you want to make over $100,000 a year, why are you talking about making money with anyone who makes under $100,000 a year?" Half the attendees' heads nod in agreement. I add: "To whom are you listening?" Just one formula I teach can help someone starting with $10,000 make $200,000-$300,000 in the next year. Loaded with enthusiasm, probably caught from me or one of my instructors, they approach their stockbroker or financial planner or even a friend or family member. Do you know what happens next? You probably do know, because this has more than likely happened to you.

Your newfound idea is shot down and usually by the flimsiest or stupidest reasons. It could be a simple, innocent question like, "Are you sure this still works?" It could be a bitter attack on the messenger.

It does not matter what the idea is. It will get shot down. Your enthusiasm is a target. Can you imagine, in the furthest stretches of your imagination, your spouse, your friend, your parents, or your stockbroker saying something like this:

"That sounds wonderful, and you're just the person to do it."

"Wow! What a great plan. Let me study up so I can help you achieve success."

"Great! Now go to town and make a million bucks."

Just think of the happiness we would have if we got this type of response. If you think success is a group affair, think again. Virtually every great achievement happens because of the passion, the drive, of one man or woman. In the history of mankind, great things do not happen by committee.

It is lonely in these roles. Don't think your friends and family will always understand. They may watch from afar and brag about you if you make it, or point fingers if you don't.

If you are on the other side of the fence, and your spouse or friend approaches you, and if you choose to use one of the above responses, make sure their life insurance policy is in force before you do. Remember they may have spent weeks (even years) preparing their presentation. They may have tried to ascertain your negative and naïve response and to think up, in advance, their answers to your questions.

It seems that the easiest thing to do in the world is to be critical, negative, or unresponsive. Sarcasm (at this time and any other) serves no purpose. Being negative is the easiest and cheapest way to be. If you're not up on something, you're down on it. Really take time out and consider your responses to others when they have a new idea or plan. Think through the influence you have on others. And then think, "what right do I have to be negative with this person?" Or, "who set me up to be judge and jury?"

A case point: when I wrote my first book on the stock market, *Wall Street Money Machine*, it hit the bestseller list. My seminars took off. Things were great, but the media and some of the financial elite criticized me. Stockbrokers everywhere told their clients that my ideas did not work. Much to their chagrin, I suppose, my students persisted. They worked the formulas. Soon brokerage firms were helping my students learn. They were buying my books and selling them or giving them away. Now, many people tell me that their brokers wait for them to call to see what they are playing so the brokers can copy them. I have students telling me that when they open a new account their brokers won't let them trade a certain way. They finally say they have been to Wade Cook's Wall Street Workshop™; and the stockbrokers welcome them in and allow them to really get going. In just two years, many of my once taboo formulas have become the standard. They're not only tolerated but also now accepted and used.

Oh, there are still those out there that think I'm on the edge, but they haven't taken the time to really read and understand my cash flow formulas. Bookstore managers tell me they often sell out of dozens of my books at a time, because brokers buy them en masse for their clients. Wow! Others see the continued sales of my books, and everyone wants in on the success. Where were they when I was being criticized? On the sidelines, like your friends, family, and future partners may be when you tell them the idea you're enthused about.

THINGS THAT WORK

I am into things that work repetitiously. I look at lives without enthusiasm or at companies lacking spirit, mission, and passion, and I think it's sad.

Give me a man or woman with enthusiasm and we'll set the world on fire. The product or service is secondary. Yes, one can have a passion for his product but the product isn't as important. It's enthusiasm that endures. An enthusiastic person finds new or better products. I have always said to bet on the jockey, not on the horse. Now that I have raised, shown, and bred horses, I will add an interesting twist: find a horse with enthusiasm, one that loves to be in the show, and you'll have a winner. There is no substitute for well-directed, sustained passion.

Experience shows that success is due less to ability than to zeal. The winner is he who gives himself to work, body and soul.

— CHARLES BUXTON

Let me tell you straight away, I know I can help you achieve a success beyond your wildest dreams if you'll just give me a chance. I positively know I can make a small, great, HUGE difference in your life. You choose. I've helped people who are in no way as smart as you. I've made a difference in people's lives who have much less money than you have. I've definitely helped people with less luck than you have. In this uphill battle to help you and do good in your life, I have a three-way challenge. I must convince you of three things:

1. **You Can Do It.** You can. I know you can. You can get rich – whatever that means to you. You can quit your job shortly. You can pay off your bills. You can pay a large tithe to your church, etc. But how? I'm glad you asked. The stock market can make a perfect part-time business. All you need is a phone. No computers, no gadgets. You don't need all the usual expenses of a regular business. Trading (not investing) has entrance and exit points (usually three to five weeks). Buy wholesale to sell retail. There are learnable, workable formulas that are really cool – because the extra cash flow lets you accomplish so much.

   These systems are not easy, but by knowledge, by practice and by a clear understanding of the components, you can work with your money and it can (YES, it will) replace your day job. Again, I'm confident you can qualify yourself for admittance back into the American Dream. I won't give up on you. If you become one of our students, you'll deserve the best fighting chance to kick your life into high gear.

2. **You Can Do It Here.** (where you are) In your back bedroom, in your car, on a coffee break, you are minutes a day from stirring up more cash flow than you can spend.

   Yes, it may be tough at first as you go through the learning curve, but believe me the results are worth it. Just imagine having hundreds of thousands of dollars waiting for your retirement.

   Look at the words of just a few of my students.

"My first option trade was four days after Microsoft announced a stock split. 11¹/₂ months after my first option trade, I've made $1,338,081.43 net profit. I originally started with $36,000 so that makes it a 3,716.89% actual increase on my investment. WOW!!"

—MYKE L., WA

"I started trading on 10-19-95 with $2,900... I recently took an account from $16,000 to $330,000 in two weeks, and $35,000 to $2,484,000 in six weeks. I made $1.25 million in one day."

—GLENN M., IL

"I had $36,000 and turned it into $460,000 in less than 3¹/₂ months. In another account, I took $100,000 and turned it into $400,000 in four weeks, and then, in another, I made $30,000 in one week for a total (account balance) of $960,000."

—JOHN T., OK

They did it, you can too. Just imagine, a free and clear house, no debts, a new car, great vacations, and being able to help others. Where would these people be if they had listened to the average stockbroker? If you keep doing what you've been doing, why would you ever expect different results? Isn't that the definition of insanity? If you want this great life, it's yours for the taking. And...just imagine doing all of this in your pajamas.

3. **You Can Do It Now.** Yes, now – in this crazy volatile market. Actually, most successful stock market traders love volatility and learn to use it to their advantage. You play the market at hand. Don't be fooled–the energy flows are real. There are fortunes being made all around you. You don't need luck, you need expertise. There is no such thing as negative energy, but you can sure do things to block positive energy. Stop it!

This next part is an excerpt from my book, *Success: American Style.*

Dare To Be Great

You, too, can achieve great things. The freedoms we enjoy provide fertile soil for achievement. There's an old proverb which says this: "The biggest fish you'll ever catch is still swimming in the ocean." It's true.

With godly genes in our spiritual blood we are destined to greatness if only we will realize our potential, act on our inspiration and perform in right ways.

Truly, it can be said, that the only thing holding us back is our own drive or lack thereof.

I hope these thoughts help you to see that you, too, can achieve whatever it is you want.

Lives of great men all remind us
We can make our lives sublime,
And, departing, leave behind us
Footprints on the sand of time;

Footprints, that perhaps another,
Sailing o'er life's solemn main,
A forlorn and shipwrecked brother,
Seeing, shall take heart again.

— Henry Wadsworth Longfellow

Get in the flow. You can't get rich on a mental desert island. Surround yourself with achievers. Lose the losers. May I humbly ask that you consider, as an alternative to the old rut you're in, a new place to go and a new group to hang out with – yes, me and my "Team Wallstreet.™" We're not perfect, but we're students first, educators second. We are doing what we teach and teaching what we do. We are always improving and all this is to your benefit.

Now, as I said before, you bring a lot of baggage on this trip. To get off the ground, we need to discard much of it. Misplaced skepticism never accomplished anything. Again, test, don't trust. I'm coming up on a major (earth/mental moving) challenge, but first this quote by Patrick James, one of the Stock Market Institute of Learning's™ instructors.

> *The person with a theory is always at the mercy of a person with an experience.*
> — PATRICK JAMES

I want you excited again! Oh, not so much excited by what we teach as by what you'll be able to *do*. The American Dream is alive and well. We're here to help you live that dream to its fullest.

Right now, I must convince you to put aside all of the mental games you play that serve you not. Read on in this chapter. You'll learn a little about the stock market, BUT you'll also learn a lot about you. I don't really need to convince you about the stock market, but I do need to convince you that "you're the one."

Respectfully: you can do so much more with me on your team. I pledge you my support, my continued quest for "cash flow" knowledge, my ongoing desire to keep improving and my faith in God and his desires of Abundance for us. Our lives can and will be so much better when we put Him first.

Do you see how tough my task is? I pose this question: if you do not believe in your own ability to succeed, will you test me to the point that you'll believe in the systems I've developed? I say trust no one (but God), test everyone.

Decide. You must. This is an important decision. The consequences of your choice will affect your life and your family's life for generations to come, or your decision will leave you alone – where you are. If where you are is where you want to be, that's great, but if where you want to be is a small or great distance from where you are, then you need a sturdy vehicle to help you get there.

I honestly think the last thing you need is more useless information. I also feel that the last thing you need in relation to the stock market is real time trades, and ignorant strategies, which get even the best traders in trouble. In addition to this, I have seen people follow stockbroker's advice into risky and even boring investments with disastrous results – setting their wealth process (nest egg) back years.

I have learned by sad experience that people who use "asset allocation" as their primary strategy suffer immensely. They need "formula allocation." All of us need to be careful of the "get-the-commission-at-any-cost" financial professional.

"Wrote Covered Calls and made an average 17% per month return. Gave control to my broker and now I'm broker. As soon as I violate Wade's rules and strategies, I start losing in the market. Now we are back on track! Thank you."

— Don G., CA

What is the difference between someone making $50,000 a year, and someone making $250,000 per year? And $2,500,000 per year? The answer is the effective use of specialized knowledge.

Following are 13 formulas that are street-tested ways to put your money to work. Check this out: even in our own accounts, the one strategy that causes us the most concern is the buy and hold – be out of control – formula. The other twelve are methods to help you quit your job. We want to help you quit your job.

When I do radio or TV talk shows, many hosts will ask me the difference between everyone else and me. The obvious answer is that they sell investments, I educate. They have stodgy old methods, which more often than not produce bad bottom lines. I share formulas for cash flow. I put the emphasis on selling, on meter-drop income (consistent predictable cash profits), on rational, logical ways to use the stock market as a business – a business that will support people and their families so they can get on with their lives.

Even within this educational process, everyone needs to realize that each of my thirteen strategies are different.

1. They have their own beginning, middle and end – entrance points and exit points.

2. Each has its own set of rules or factors which make it work.

3. Each has a specific time to be used and only works or works best at that time – or market occurrence.

Coming up will be the strategy, a brief definition or explanation, *when* it is to be used and *who* should use it. Remember, the "why" is usually more important than the "how."

Strategy #1: Blue Chips (Right–Term Hold)

What: Use fundamentals and technical analysis to find great stocks in companies with likelihood of going up for your future. May be used for Writing Covered Calls. Sold when profitable for extra cash. Many of these may pay dividends.

When: Anytime. My other strategies are more income generation oriented, so you can pay off debt, pay the bills and then invest in these nice (safe?) stocks. Don't be afraid to clean house. Build your own "Mutual Fund."

Who: Start young. Add to positions as you go. Monitor your account to make sure you have the best. Great for gifts and gifting and donations to your church. *Note: See Semester Investor.*

Strategy #2: Rolling Stock™

What: A system of buying and selling less expensive stocks – trading in a sideways pattern – buy at $2 (support) sell at $3 (resistance) in repeated waves. Look at the charts on the following pages for examples.

When: In a flat market, or sideways moving stock. Even in good markets, many stocks move in rolling patterns.

Who: Beginners. Those who want little risk, and not huge, but consistent profits.

MEDEMICUS

GRUPO ELEKTRA SA DE OV

GREKA ENERGY

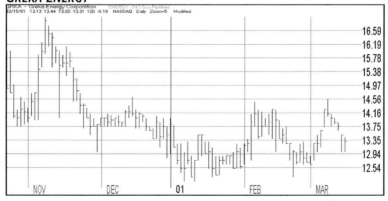

HUFFY

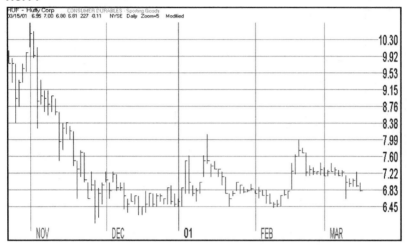

STRATEGY #3: OPTIONS

What: Use small amounts of money on low-cost, limited risk options to control large blocks of stocks. A movement in stock from $84 to $88 could see the $80 call option move from $6 to $8, i.e., $6,000 to $8,000 in hours, days or weeks. Upside potential is huge, loss limited to premium paid.

When: Use calls on up movements, puts on down movements. Risky, should be practice traded. Huge profit potential – available and workable in all markets. Added risk: options expiration dates.

Who: People who do research, understand connections and power of news and potential news (rumors). Those who want large, quick profits. Note: only use small "risk" capital.

STRATEGY #4: WRITING COVERED CALLS

What: Sell options (generate income in one day) against your stock positions – agreeing to sell stock at predetermined price (profits). Nice monthly cash flow machine–10%-15% possible cash income–per month. More, if stock is on margin.

When: Used on large stocks–with options. Used anytime to pick up cash and then sell stock or keep it depending on the strike price–"Do you really want to sell the stock?"

Who: People who want income. $100,000 in stocks will produce $10,000 to $15,000 of extra income. Many beginners buy stock just to sell calls for income.

STRATEGY #5: STOCK SPLITS

What: Many companies split their stocks when they get pricey. If good, company stocks have tendency to go back up to or above price before split: Sometimes in two to five years, sometimes in three to nine months. Look at the following charts.

When: Five times to get in and out. Build a portfolio of these stocks with limits of doing splits or quick-turns. Options trading on these enhance potential and possibly reduce risk.

Who: Anyone needing profits. These are easy to practice and master before using real money. Many one to three day trades available.

EMULEX

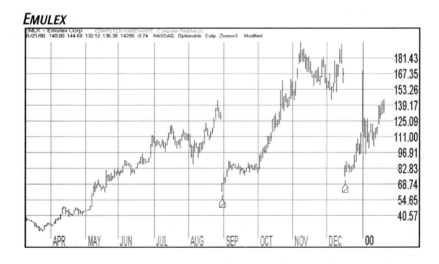

XILINX

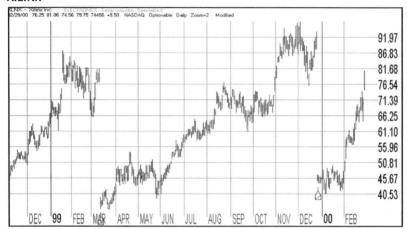

EMC

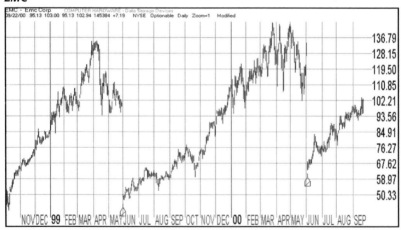

STRATEGY #6: SELLING PUTS

What: Generate income by agreeing to have a stock sold to you at a price you like–on a company you like. Nice income, plus potential to buy stock wholesale. Seems risky to naíve stockbrokers, who, ironically, will sell you risky stocks in a heartbeat.

When: Use in bullish situations. Stay above strike price and consider your margin requirements. Note: a variation of this is the Bull Put Spread to eliminate much of the risk and lower margin.

Who: Those who want cash flow. Can be as safe as someone wants, depending on stock choices and option strike prices.

STRATEGY #7: BULL CALL SPREADS

What: Similar to Writing Covered Calls, but use purchase of call option (much less money) rather than stock. Limits risk, and by selling upper calls you limit profits. Spreads are created when you buy a call and sell a call on the same stock at different strike prices.

When: Can be done repetitiously. Good in any market—works best with up-trending stock. Huge profits (more risk) in high-flying stocks.

Who: Good for cautious people. Could generate 15% to 30% cash, three to four week returns.

STRATEGY #8: BULL PUT SPREADS

What: This is my favorite. It's a credit spread, which means you get paid to put it in place. You sell a put (income) and buy a put (outgo) below the price of the stock on a Bullish stock. Stock stays above strike price, and you keep the cash.

When: New definition of Bullish: the stock goes up, or at least stays up above a certain strike price. Used when stocks hit support, or on bounce (dip). Note: use a Bear Call Spread on opposite—downtrends.

Who: People who want monthly income. 20% to 40% two to four week actual cash returns are very common.

STRATEGY #9: ROLLING OPTIONS™

What: Same as Rolling Stock, but on more expensive stocks. As a stock hits resistance and starts up, buy a call, then at its peak buy a put; or do Bull Put Spreads on upswings and Bear Call Spreads on downturns.

When: These are available every day. You must grasp option volatility and pricing. You need at least $5 to $10 swings in the stock.

Who: People who have extra time to monitor positions, or get adept at placing sell orders. Good money-maker.

STRATEGY #10: BARGAIN HUNTING, TURNAROUNDS AND BOTTOM FISHING

What: Buying low priced stocks on serious dips, check fundamentals and buy stock or options on stock. Try for doubles and practice, practice, practice. Use extreme caution with penny stocks.

When: When stocks fall out of favor, and take on new management, company comes up with new products, ends lawsuits, or is a takeover candidate.

Who: People should use limited money here–profits are spectacular, but few and far between. Expertise can be developed.

STRATEGY #11: RANGE RIDERS

What: Similar to Rolling Stocks, but with upward trend. Use trend lines (and/or support lines) for entrance points. Place sell orders to exit trades with 20% to 40% profits. Use stop loss to minimize losses (risk).

When: Many stocks follow this pattern. Can be played with stock or options. Spreads are also effective here. Reverse range riders can be used when stock moves in opposite (down) patterns.

Who: People with time to monitor positions. Nice two to three day trades available. Also, trader should subscribe to a charting service for support lines, trend lines and moving averages.

STRATEGY #12: INITIAL PUBLIC OFFERINGS (IPOS)

What: Invest in stocks in a 'PRE', on the 'OPEN', or 'POST' IPO formula. Each has concerns and definite exit points. Tough to do on the open–consider 25 day IPO rule (quiet period) and jump in there. These stocks are highly volatile. There are probably better times.

When: Obviously, when a company is ready to, or is going public. Watch local newspapers. There are many times to get in. Don't let ads (fads) on TV, affect you. It can be difficult to make money with IPOs.

Who: People who like a challenge and added risk–must do extra homework and be above the hype.

Strategy #13: Spin-Offs

What: Good opportunity to get in on a company with a market niche, good management with a lot to prove. Great examples abound. Best play is on the company (BABY) being spun-off, not the parent. (Unless parent is generating a lot of cash.)

When: This is a rarely-used strategy because there just aren't that many available, but great when available. Buy stocks, options, or do spreads.

Who: People who like a lot of safety–even then, one must be careful. There are many ways to play these. Often options aren't available for several months.

Summary

There you have it. A complete package. What do you need? Income? Safety? Monthly Cash Flow? Growth? Bigger Profits?

Again, we share – you learn and earn.

I probably have offended every stockbroker and financial professional in the country. Most of these people, who you think would be up on these cash flow methods, know little about them. When this cab driver took on Wall Street, I had no idea what a commotion I'd cause. I'll apologize to them in advance, and invite them to attend the Wall Street Workshop. We should charge them double to pay for all the anguish they've caused people. Profits are waiting. All you have to do is grasp the knowledge, gain an understanding, and apply it for profits.

Consider what everyone gets out of this. Brokers get commissions. I get book royalties. You get profits today and more profits tomorrow. You actually take control of your financial destiny. You. You and only you. No one will learn and understand your financial situation like <u>you</u>.

You have choices. One is to keep trading your time for money; the other is to put your knowledge to work and get your money to work as hard as you do–even harder. Expect more from your money, learn what it takes and then get more *from* your money.

MARKET CONDITION	Zero to Zillions Home Study Course	Blue Chip Trading	Rolling Stock	Options (Calls & Puts)	Stock Splits	Writing Covered Calls	Selling Puts	Bull Put Spreads	Bull Call Spreads	Bargain Hunting/Turnarounds	Wall Street Workshop	IPOs	Spin Offs	Rolling Options	Range Riders	W.I.N. – Internet Tutorial Service
Whole Market Bullish	•	•	•	•	•	•	•	•	•	•	•	•	•	•	•	•
Whole Market Bearish	•			•							•		•	•		•
Sector Moves	•	•		•	•	•	•	•	•		•		•	•	•	•
Hi-Tech Trades	•	•		•	•	•	•	•			•	•		•		•
Low-Tech Trades	•	•	•	•			•	•	•	•	•	•		•	•	•
Stock – going up	•	•		•	•		•	•	•		•				•	•
Stock – going down	•			•		•		•		•	•			•		•
Stock – going sideways	•		•	•		•		•	•		•			•		•

YOUR CONDITION

YOUR CONDITION	Zero to Zillions Home Study Course	Blue Chip Trading	Rolling Stock	Options (Calls & Puts)	Stock Splits	Writing Covered Calls	Selling Puts	Bull Put Spreads	Bull Call Spreads	Bargain Hunting/Turnarounds	Wall Street Workshop	IPOs	Spin Offs	Rolling Options	Range Riders	W.I.N. – Internet Tutorial Service
I need cash	•		•		•						•	•				•
I need steady income	•		•		•						•					•
I need growth	•	•			•	•				•	•	•	•			•
More safety	•	•	•			•					•		•			•
More risk, more profits	•			•			•			•	•	•		•	•	•
Little time to trade	•	•	•			•		•			•					•
Quick Turn Profits	•		•	•	•			•	•		•	•	•	•		•
Retirement income	•	•	•	•		•		•	•		•			•		•

On the previous page is a matrix. Find yourself – your risk/reward tolerance, cash flow needs, safety requirements and future growth needs; then look at market conditions and movement and see what it takes to gain an expertise so you get the results you want.

Following is an excerpt from Special Report #714, Soar With Eagles: Attitude is Everything:

HOW TO GET AND KEEP A GREAT ATTITUDE

Are there methods that will keep your attitudes high? There are, but first a choice needs to be made. From the way I see it, you have two ways to get and keep a positive attitude. One is from external sources and the other from somewhere internal. Let's explore each. Don't fudge here on which one you need.

External. Is it always something outside yourself which gets you pumped up? Do you need pep rallies and pep talks? Do you need friends to pat you on the back and to constantly encourage you? Do you need motivational books and tapes to keep you going? Now, don't get me wrong, all of these things have their place. But you've got to decide what it is that makes you tick. Contrast all of this external feedback to the following:

Internal. Are you naturally positive? Do you find the best even in bad situations? Does external feedback just add to your good attitude? Do you get back up when you get knocked down? Do you feel that you could write a book on having a good attitude and inspiring others? Are you sought out by others for help, encouragement and a pat on the back?

The choice between external and internal is easy but loaded with consequences. If you're in need of external stimuli, admit it, and then seek the best help you can. Most people fall into this category. I submit that you'll be happier if you are an internal person. Your radiance will shine, your attitude will exude out of you. You will be peaceful with yourself–with who you are. God's words have an incredible effect on you. We all have a spark of the divine within us. Your light shines because you're excited about something.

As I said, the choice is simple: external or internal, but then the work needed to achieve desired results will be different. I'll assume that you want to move in the direction of being internally motivated. It's rare, but so much less expensive than paying for all the external "stuff."

An Attitude of Gratitude. Live with a thankful heart. Express your thanks often and in many situations. You will garner to you like minded people.

Our Attitude Does Determine Our Altitude. Have an attitude of working a plan, getting educated and associating with good people. If you're mired down in the pits, you need to check your attitude. Let's not expect a high altitude without a high attitude.

What we all need is more vitality, more exuberance and enthusiasm. We don't need to be boisterous, pushy or manipulative–and attitude makes all the difference in the world. Our attitude determines who our friends will be. Our attitude determines what grades we'll get.

Our attitude determines what kind of a relationship we'll have with our spouse, our children, our friends. Our altitude determines how we'll react to God's Word.

Attitude determines our course of action, our resolve and therefore our destination.

The attitude you take towards problems and difficulties is far and away the most important factor in controlling and mastering them.
— Norman Vincent Peale

Below is an excerpt from *Soar With Eagles, Special Report #722, Wealth: A Generous Viewpoint:*

I've used Proverbs 13:20 to show people how important it is to seek out wise people and "walk with them." Also, by contrast, how hanging out with foolish, ignorant or negative people can be so detrimental. The verse says this:

He that walketh with wise men shall be wise: but a companion of fools shall be destroyed.

PROVERBS 13:20.

Rabbi Hama in the Talmud states that poverty is as bad on a household as fifty diseases. Many Jews throughout history were extremely poor, but as the rabbis said:

Poverty is one of three things that drive a person crazy.

TALMUD, ER 41B

They instructed the people to work, to seek gainful employment; to move to another town if need be, but support your family. This was given as mitzvah, or by way of command. This is why so many work so hard.

Conversely, wealth can also be detrimental. People get caught up in it and think they're something special:

If you have money, you are wise, handsome, and you also sing well.

— ANONYMOUS

F. Scott Fitzgerald indeed said, "The rich are different." Wealth can cause people to think they can get away with bending the rules – rules they impose on others. This is a common occurrence with politicians, who acquire wealth and power.

Mother Theresa and many others take vows of poverty. All they do, all they have, is for the poor. To them, this is good. Others do not go to this extreme, yet live fruitful and charity laden lives. Again, it's all in the attitude. The spirit truly softens the heart. Read again verse seven:

There is that maketh himself rich, yet hath nothing: there is that maketh himself poor, yet hath great riches.

PROVERBS 13:7

I know people like this. They are rich because of a good wife, loving children, enough food and clothing. They are truly happy. They are content even though they don't have abundance. Others give all away, and find a different kind of richness.

3 PLEASING WAYS

As we move through life conducting our business, guiding our careers, and finding ourselves up and down on the peaks and valleys of wealth, we should develop a right attitude. We cannot be proud, without corresponding consequences. We cannot be self-pitying without developing a grumbling, attitude of smallness. We cannot do bad and expect good.

When a man's ways please the LORD, he maketh even his enemies to be at peace with him.

PROVERBS 16:7.

I for one have been rich and poor. Of course, rich feels better. But I'd give it all up to continue my relationship with God, if that's what He desired of me. I've been blessed beyond measure, but when my life is right, or when I'm changing to make it right, then do I find peace and comfort.

Better is a little with righteousness than great revenues without right.

PROVERBS 16:8.

Our own thinking process will cause us to choose this business or that one – this course or that course. We are all so very different. What a boring world it would be if everyone wanted to be x-ray technicians. Once we've chosen our path, let's let God set our feet in proper values and guide our steps – or the way we handle our affairs.

A man's heart deviseth his way: but the LORD directeth his steps.

PROVERBS 16:9

We control our thoughts and by so doing control our future. Will it be one of good enterprise, or one of wasted talents? Will we be all we can be, and be what God wants us to be, or will pride, stubbornness and bad actions divert our attention?

4

INCREASE YOUR POWERS OF OBSERVATION

It was just one of those mornings: away from home, busy getting ready to teach a seminar. And then out of the blue I heard something on television which stopped me in my tracks. I went to the edge of the bed and sat less than five feet from the screen. It was an HBO movie about the life of Galileo.

Galileo, a scientist famous even in his own time, was given charge of the Prince. The Queen wanted him straightened out. He learned slowly but soon became fascinated by the art of discovery. He was learning at the feet of the great master. In this one scene, Galileo was teaching the form or method of observation.

He said (and I'm paraphrasing) that it all starts with observing something. This observation causes thought – maybe wonder or concern – but thought. The pondering starts. Then one is to notice trends, effects and relationships. From this one forms a guess, a hypothesis. This hypothesis then is tested, observed, tested again, and finally a law is developed and set forth.

I was fascinated by these thoughts. They hit home to me. I felt like I was among friends, though they were characters in a TV movie. This was much more than just an occasion of serendipity. Serendipity is a happy, joyous or worthwhile discovery you make on the way to something else. I'm sure Galileo had many discoveries which were made by accident or by observation, and serendipity has affected my life so many times that it is hard to count.

The connection here was that I had discovered the same process in several financial arenas. With cash flow as my primary motive I moved from real estate to business to the stock market. My design was to figure out ways to put the marketplace to work for me. If it was cash flow I needed, then that's where I would start.

I originally observed that money is made when something is sold. In real estate, the selling was much easier if the property was bought right in the first place. Bought right. What does that mean? When you go to sell a property (or rent it) you want all of your options open. You want the process to be easy and fast. If you overpaid for the property, or even paid market price, then to rapidly resell would be difficult. You'll have to build in more value or wait for inflation.

If you put too much cash in, either in the form of the down payment or in fix-up money, then to recover this cash you need to sell a certain way. Your selling opportunities are limited.

If the loans you either assumed or created are difficult, for instance if they have a due on sale clause, then once again a few doors to selling have slammed closed.

In short, buying right means that you buy wholesale—get a property underpriced or with a lot of potential value. Limit your fix-up cash and down payment. Only assume loans which can be re-assumed or taken over by the next guy. Add it all up and a quick sale for a nice profit can occur.

Before I move on, a point. Many people reading this are thinking, "Not very many properties fit this model." You're right. Out of 100 houses, three or four will work for me. So why waste time on the 97 out of 100 which do not fit my model? Remember, work the formulas. Get good at finding the 3 that work.

I've outlined this whole process in my books *Real Estate Money Machine* and *Real Estate for Real People*. By the way, one result I observed and have shouted from the rooftops is the perpetual cash flow results. Once you work real estate my way the monthly payments keep coming in for 20 to 30 years. Even in my stock market seminars I mention the process: two-step your money away from the market. It's too risky. Put your money (profits) in other investments like real estate or other business interests. Buy second mortgages. Real estate paper is debt owed to you, debt with monthly checks which you live on. (See my course on buying and selling mortgages and deeds of trust called *Paper Tigers*.)

Now back to the stock market. The comparison to real estate can only go so far, but the selling comparison is vital to understand. My observation in the stock market is essentially the same. You make money, actual cash profit, when you sell something. Many people reading this don't need extra cash. Their existing job or business produces their livelihood. It's not to them that I wish to address these next remarks. I'll try to kill two birds with one stone.

Most of my students come to learn how to make money. They don't necessarily want to or need to replace existing income; they want to add to it. They want more money. They'll worry about retiring later. They have families to raise, older parents to support, kids to put through college, *et cetera*.

The aim is to cash-flow the stock market. More specifically, to use what little cash they have to generate an extra $2,000 to $6,000 per month. That amount of extra cash will make a substantial difference in their lives. They have only $5,000 to start with, so the task is monumental.

Can you imagine walking into a stockbroker's office and saying something like this, "I've got $15,000. Will you help me have it produce $4,000 a month?" Then the broker replies, "Sure, let's put it in ATT or this XYZ mutual fund." Dream on. It won't happen.

What's the alternative? This is where my critics get all bent out of shape. To me it's the same as my real estate days. Yes, you can own stocks. They grow in value or not. You're out of control. Let's say you select wisely, and in time for retirement you've built up a nice nest egg. Way to go.

But what if you need income now? What if your husband is hurt and can't work? What about death, divorce and disaster – the three

Ds? Just like real estate, the cash is made when you sell something. Why not buy stocks when they are low and sell when high? Take some money and pay the bills. It was a simple observation. Simple but with far-reaching dynamics.

And if you add options, the party picks up. Before that observation a quote by George Bernard Shaw:

> *When I was a young man I observed that nine out of ten things I did were failures. I didn't want to be a failure, so I did ten times more work.*
>
> — GEORGE BERNARD SHAW

Options become a workhorse. A $4 call option on an $80 stock can double with even a 6% to 7% move in the stock. Selling options on stock you own generates income. Rolling options on peaks and valleys provides a double whammy. Using spreads with options reduces risk and generates income.

I've learned these plays in my never-ending search for safe cash flow. This observation sprouts new branches daily. The roots keep spreading. Lately I've observed a remarkable phenomenon in regards to "newsy-type" periods around quarterly and annual filings.

Let me share with you several of these observations which I hope will make you a better trader.

1. Those who succeed are those who put blinders on to distractions. They get good, indeed they become an expert in a certain type of trade. They know it cold. They know the best entrance points and the best sell points. They know the strategy so they know when to cut their losses. "Knowledge is power" is not a cliché, but a way of life. They work themselves.

> *One of the strongest characteristics of genius is the power of lighting its own fire.*
>
> — JOHN FOSTER

They can hardly wait to get out of bed in the morning because their path is laid out through good habits. Yes, they explore new things and one day a new strategy may replace their mainstay income producer, but until that day they are faithful to the process–always improving, always advancing.

> *Responsibilities gravitate to the person who can shoulder them; power flows to the man or woman who knows how.*
>
> — ELBERT HUBBARD

2. To stay successful one must love what he is doing. How else, with the tediousness that every job involves, will a person progress and improve?

How sad it is to see one who is miserable with their work. Let me share with you a few verses out of Ecclesiastes, Chapter 2. This is a sad person indeed. But keep reading–the pivotal verse is Verse 24.

18 *Yea, I hated all my labour which I had taken under the sun; because I should leave it unto the man that shall be after me.*

19 *And who knoweth whether he shall be a wise man or a fool? Yet shall he have rule over all my labour wherein I have laboured, and wherein I have shewed myself wise under the sun. This is also vanity.*

20 *Therefore I went about to cause my heart to despair of all the labour which I took under the sun.*

21 *For there is a man whose labour is in wisdom and in knowledge, and in equity; yet to a man that hath not laboured therein shall he leave it for his portion. This also is vanity and a great evil.*

22 *For what hath man of all his labour, and of the vexation of his heart, wherein he hath laboured under the sun?*

23 *For all his days are sorrows and his travail grief; yea, his heart taketh not rest in the night. This is also vanity.*

24 *There is nothing better for a man, than that he should eat and drink, and that he should make his soul enjoy good in his labour. This also I saw, that it was from the hand of God.*

26 *For God giveth to a man that is good in his sight wisdom,
and knowledge, and joy; but to the sinner he giveth travail,
to gather and to heap up, that he may give to him that is
good before God...*

— Ecclesiastes, Chapter 2

If God wants us to be happy, who are we to countermand Him? Now, happy at what? I've never really thought that "working the market" could be fun. At least I've never thought that I would teach the market—and my style of trading—as a fun process, one to be enjoyed. I thought that people only wanted results—more cash flow. But alas, I underestimated thousands of my students.

People only see what they are prepared to see.

— Ralph Waldo Emerson

They love the market. The machinations, the suspense and mystery. They love the cash flow results, because of what they can do with the money. Look at a few of these crazy testimonials I get in.

"This workshop gave me the first hand, real time experience to see these strategies put to the test. This was absolutely exciting!!"

— Jeffery Lowe

"These are literally life-changing strategies. I know that I can never look at investing in the same light again."

— Kevin Sullivan

"What a wonderful gift I gave myself when I decided to learn something new and put my money for the classes and my energy behind strategies that were all new. Thank you Wade, for making all the strategies available and in a language and format I could understand."

— Virginia Haas

Now back to you. Maybe you don't enjoy the stock market like these people. That's okay. Do what makes you happy and fulfilled.

The market–stocks, options, margin, spreads, stock splits–is not for everyone. As a matter of fact, I think you've got to have your blood cell count a little off to really enjoy it. If it's not your cup of tea, you probably won't have the patience, persistence and dedication to excel. You'd be better off finding and doing something you enjoy.

However, if you like the market, go to the section on strategies and find an area that you love. Work it. Excel at it.

> *What we love to do we find time to do.*
> — John Lancaster Spalding

There are not enough hours in a day to make all the mistakes you'll need to make to learn each market's lesson. It truly is a wise person who learns from others. Read, attend seminars, question your brokers, talk to others who are walking the walk.

> *Nothing is more terrible than ignorance in action.*
> — Goethe

Let me put in a plug here for the Semper Financial™ Investors Educational Convention. These conventions are large and powerful. Tell me where else you can go for three days and listen to and question 15 to 20 authors and instructors? Tell me where else you can visit with hundreds of attendees who are doing the deals? There is no place other then a Semper Financial™ Convention. If I were you, I'd go to at least three or four per year.

Sometimes you get so busy your saw becomes dull. Take time out to sharpen your saw.

3. People seem to be trying to use machines in every aspect of life to make things better. Computers are machines. I'll stick with people–as imperfect, irrational and wonderful as they are.

> *One machine can do the work of fifty ordinary men.*
> *No machine can do the work of one extraordinary man.*
> — Elbert Hubbard

Next to learning from others is choosing a team of professionals to help you: CPAs and attorneys who are business oriented (pros who are walking the walk).

> *However learned or eloquent, man knows nothing truly that he has not learned from experience.*
> — CHRISTOPHER MARTIN WIELAND

A good stockbroker is essential. I'm not big into online trading. It costs too much. A good broker will make you money, not cost you. In one trade this year that my broker brought me I made enough profits to pay all of his commissions for three to four months. I pity the person who tries to go it alone. His reward: bad order fills, missed opportunities and less fun.

> *The knowledge of the world is only to be acquired in the world and not in a closet.*
> — PHILLIP CHESTERFIELD

4. My stockbroker taught me a spring/summer observation about doing stocks. Look about – see connections. Notice things. Try, test, improve, form patterns. For the past several years drug stocks have hit the winter doldrums about May and then into June and July many of these stocks surge forward. Why not play options on them?

    Look at the run up in Merck & Co., in May and June. Many FDA approvals come out in June, before summer vacations. With Pfizer, notice strong growth. Look at the spring increase even before May and June.

MERCK

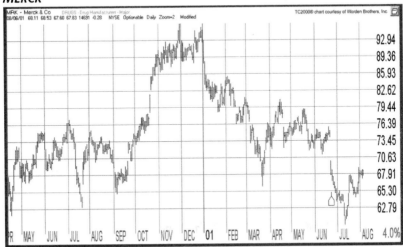

PFIZER

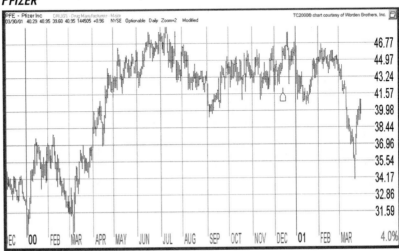

Also note that there is an index of these stocks, ticker DRG. Look at the comparison of these yearly charts for 1995-98.

1995 PHARMACEUTICAL INDEX

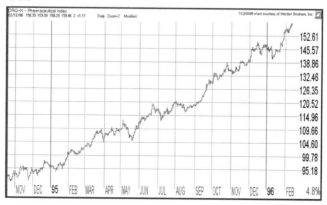

1996 PHARMACEUTICAL INDEX

1997 PHARMACEUTICAL INDEX

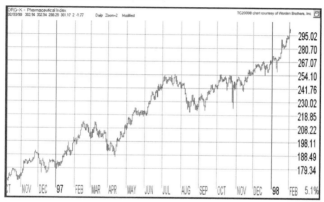

1998 Pharmaceutical Index

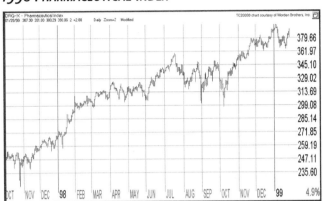

This is an index of many pharmaceuticals. Notice the April/May run ups. Then look how these performed into the end of the year.

So I've played all of them recently. Wow, four years they've performed this way. Will it continue next year? Who knows?

This index is made up of the following stocks. Are there other plays?

1.	ABT	ABBOTT LABS
2.	AZA	ALZA CORPORATION
3.	AHP	AMER HOME PRODS
4.	AMGN	UQ AMGEN INC.
5.	AZN	ASTRAZENECA – ADR
6.	BMY	BRISTOL-MYER SQB
7.	GLX	GLAXO WELLCO-ADR
8.	JNJ	JOHNSON & JOHNSON
9.	LLY	LILLY (ELI)
10.	MRK	MERCK & CO.
11.	PFE	PFIZER INC.
12.	PNU	PHARMACIA & UPJO
13.	SGP	SCHERING-PLOUGH
14.	SBH	SMITHKLINE B-ADR
15.	WLA	WARNER-LAMBERT

Again, notice things. Can this May effect also be part of the Red Light, Green Light May effect?

Connect the dots. What can you play before, during and as these advancing periods end?

> *He hazardeth much who depends for his learning on experience. – An unhappy master is he who is made wise only by many shipwrecks; a miserable merchant, who is neither rich nor wise till he has been bankrupt. – By experience we find out a short way instead of a long wandering.*
>
> — ROGER ASCHAM

5. Be still, take time out. Quit the busy-ness. It is wonderful to take time out. Stop. Sit still. Ponder. Our brain needs time to think, to sort things out. I wrote about this in *Business Buy The Bible*. I'll use one scripture from that section: "Be still and know that I am God."

You will make more money and for a longer period if you will just take a time out. Relaxation is therapeutic.

> *For him who has no concentration, there is no tranquility.*
>
> — BHAGAVAD GITA

> *To do great work a man must be very idle as well as very industrious.*
>
> — SAMUEL BALL

I see people becoming slaves to the process. Listen to my audio CD, *Job Free Income*. I bring up an angle of day trading (the new definition) which I think can be hurtful. We do not want the process to kill us, or even kill our ambitions. If we let it wear on us, it will wear us out.

I love my mornings. My drive time to play basketball and home again (a total of 70 to 80 minutes) is my time with my stockbrokers. One in particular has a real handle on what I like to do. He's very astute; I learn a lot from him. Once I get home, shower and head to the office my time is taken away with running a company. On a typical day, I may spend seven to ten more minutes with him before the market closes.

Sometimes I just sit and think. He's looking up prices of stocks or scrolling out to get an option quote. I sit and meditate. When I get too busy, I tire. When I tire, I make mistakes and do not enjoy the process. I, you, we all need rest – at least a frequent respite.

> *To be idle requires a strong sense of personal identity.*
> – ROBERT LOUIS STEVENSON

Your most important area of observation – one where you *need* to connect the dots – is in what you need; what your body, mind and soul need. Take care, and be wise.

6. This last point will come full circle back to #1. Never, Never, Never Quit. Don't even begin to go down the path of despair. Negativism is poison. Please read this quote.

> *Optimism is a medicine. Pessimism is a poison. Admittedly, every businessman must be realistic. He must gather facts, analyze them candidly and strive to draw logical conclusions, whether favorable or unfavorable. He must not engage in self-delusion. He must not view everything through rose-colored glasses. Granting this, the incontestable truth is that America has been built up by optimists. Not by pessimists, but by men possessing courage, confidence in the nation's destiny, by men willing to adventure, to shoulder risks terrifying to the timid.*
> – B.C. FORBES

Optimism produces opportunities. Yes, it is easy to be optimistic when one has many opportunities, but it's a question of the chicken or the egg. I submit to you that your attitude determines everything.

> *Every noble activity makes room for itself.*
> – RALPH WALDO EMERSON

Walk the walk. Get good AS you go. Production towards perfection.

Our deeds determine us, as much as we determine our deeds.

— GEORGE ELIOT

Optimism, options — opportunities. Connect the dots.

Men are not judged by their looks, habit, and appearances; but by the character of their lives and conversations, and by their works. 'Tis better that a man's own works than that another man's words should praise him.

— SIR ROGER L'ESTRANGE

NEVER QUIT

When things go wrong as they sometimes will,
when the road you're trudging seems all uphill,
when the funds are low and the debts are high,
and you want to smile buy you have to sigh,

When care is pressing you down a bit,
rest if you must but don't you quit.
Life is queer with its twists and turns,
as every one of us sometimes learns,
and many a failure turns about...
when he might have won had he stuck it out:
Don't give up though the pace seems slow...
you may succeed with another blow.

Success is failure turned inside out...
the silver tint of the clouds of doubt,
and you never can tell just how close you are...
it may be near when it seems so far:
so stick to the fight when you're hardest hit...
it's when things seem worst that you must not quit.

— AUTHOR UNKNOWN

5

RED LIGHT, GREEN LIGHT PERIODS FOR CASH FLOW

This chapter is about trading wisely. I will take several of my cash flow formulas and put them into the Red Light, Green Light perspective. You will see better times to get involved, or stay out. You will also see better times to clear out of the position based on the anticipation of movements.

Read carefully any W.I.N. updates or transaction explanations from myself, my staff or your fellow students.

In this chapter, we will cover:

1. ☐ Blue Chip
2. ☑ Rolling Stock
3. ☑ Options
4. ☑ Writing Covered Calls
5. ☐ Stock Splits
6. ☐ Selling Puts
7. ☐ Bull Call Spreads
8. ☐ Bull Put Spreads
9. ☐ Rolling Options
10. ☐ Bargain Hunting/Turnarounds
11. ☐ Range Riders
12. ☐ IPOs
13. ☐ Spin-offs
14. ☑ Updates
15. ☑ Other: Straddles

Here's to more prosperous trading!

RLGL ROLLING STOCK

A rolling stock is a stock that moves up and down in a sideways pattern. The stock finds semi-predictable support levels at the bottom, and conversely, resistance levels at the top of its price range. We look for patterns in less expensive stocks, say under $10, and look for repeatable waves.

Repeated waves of high and low points of these inexpensive rolling stocks is usually not a function of earnings announcements or pre-announcements. These movements are based on what experts call technical indicators: support and resistance levels, money flows, and a variety of news types of events.

The question is, how does this fit in with typical RLGL periods? The answer, from my experience, is the movements of these rolling stocks are helped along with up and down market movements. The movements help. Also, in down markets the stocks go down faster. In short, the roll ranges do not solely rely on market movements, but are aided along by the market in general.

The trading point is to trade the market at hand. Don't fight it. Use it. If you have a rolling stock that goes between a $2 and $3 range, and the pattern is, say a five-week roll period, but it currently seems stuck at $1.85, the ticket might be the upcoming end of the May/June Red Light period. You know as soon as you sell it early it will run right up to $3. It's not that it's totally in a lull, but it needs a little help from its friends. Sometimes, patience is the virtue needed. You can lose out on just as many profits by selling early; so why not check the calendar?

To gain a little wisdom, rethink your buy points and roll ranges. Think of compelling reasons. Rethink the storyline: Has it played out? Is the game over?

The following three charts are examples:

NEPRO BIOTHERAPEUTICS

Note: (A) Notice the downturn in December is a major part of the Red Light/Green Light scenario, (B) then the rally into year end. Even with rolling stocks, these Red Light, Green Light moves play out or exaggerate the move.

DAVE & BUSTER'S, INC.

(C) Note the weak February's in both charts.

HOMEBASE

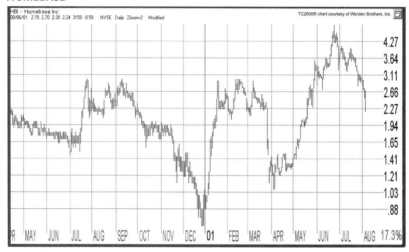

RLGL RANGE RIDERS

I'll let the pictures do the talking. Range riders are a stock movement like rolling stock, but with an upward bias. Say like this:

IBM

JUNIPER NETWORKS

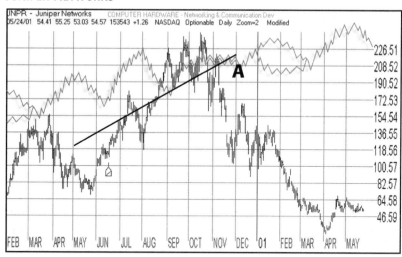

MICROSOFT

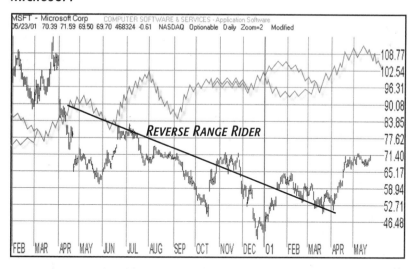

We like higher highs and higher lows. The point of this discussion is to view the charts on top of a typical RLGL movement by calendar quarters. Above is a typical chart I use from my seminars.

The solid gray is the RLGL line. The bar chart represents the stock price.

Again, everything (news, reports, sector moves) is important. Make decisions based on a variety of contrasting opinions.

RLGL OPTIONS

The right to buy or sell stock, or gamble on which way an index will move, is tied up in an option. I call them low-cost, limited risk options, because in some ways they are safer than stocks. Buying an option gives you unlimited upside potential (sort of) with limited downside risk.

Options definitely have their place, though this place in your portfolio should be limited. I think the amount of your money to tie up in owning options (not selling) should be 2% to 4%, and only up to 10% if you're very rich and don't care at all about losing money. That person is rare, so keep your options positions to a bare minimum. Options have an additional element of risk; they expire. This expiration time works against you if you purchase a call or put option. This same expiration date may work to your benefit if you're a seller of the option.

Because of this expiration date, the RLGL periods are more important. Think of it: a stock, if purchased at a bad price, might be forgiving if you have enough time. An option can easily expire before the stock can move in the way you'd hoped. The short term expiration dates give you a bigger bang for your buck on short term moves, but conversely, the short term may not allow enough time for the stock, and therefore the option, to recover.

Options present many opportunities but are also fraught with concerns. The point is to *know your exit*, either a percentage move or a dollar move. Don't ever get involved unless you know when you are going to get uninvolved.

Know the compelling reasons for the stock to move – if the stock doesn't move the right way, the option will die on you.

RLGL STRADDLES

A straddle is a variation of an option play. We've found a fair amount of success playing straddles (and strangles) into the earnings announcements. Remember the anticipation can often drive a stock up or down more than the actual earnings announcement.

The whole RLGL phenomenon is based on news and the lack of news. A stock is at $60. It is two days before the actual earnings announcement. The straddle (pure) is to buy the $60 call and the $60 put. The call is $3, the put is $2.50. If we buy both, it will cost $5.50. Ten contracts will be $5,500. Now to make money we just need a big move either way. We don't necessarily have to make money on both sides of the position. If the stock rallies into the announcement, say to $67, the call option could move to $9, or $9,000. That would be a $3,500 profit. We could sell the put for 50¢, or $500. We'll use that to cover commission and go to a movie. But, what if we just hold the put? The announcement is made. They beat their numbers, but warn of slower sales. The stock at $67 tumbles to $56 and the put is now at $5. Just $5,000 more and we have an awesome trade. If you can get both sides at a profit, then it's gravy. Enjoy the meal and move on.

A strangle is put into place if we buy the $65 call and also buy the $55 put. Why? Because they're cheaper. The $65 put is just $1.50, or $1,500 for ten contracts. The $65 call is $2, or $2,000. We now have $3,500 tied up and need a fairly good move one way or the other. If the stock doesn't move, we lose. If it goes up $5 or $6, we do well with the calls. A down movement causes a profit in the puts. This is designed to be a two to five day trade, but one side might be kept in place for two to four weeks – even just before the expiration date. We sell the remaining position at that time.

Think of this. The call could be aided by the start of the Green Light period and, once ended, the down movement, aided by the lack of news, helps the put.

I must add the following: straddles and strangles are for times when you just don't know which way the stock will move. If you truly believe the stock will rise (or fall) then it's a waste of money to buy the second side. Do your homework and play your intuition.

EXCERPT FROM *W.I.N.*

I want to address the issue of Straddles for a moment. We are coming into the earnings season and I think that playing Straddles when companies are getting ready to announce earnings reports, allows you plenty of opportunities. At least start paper trading them.

Let's talk about XYZ Company at $78. It is fairly volatile between $72 and $85. The whisper numbers say it is going to make or even beat its numbers by a small amount. You just absolutely do not know which way it is going to go. In this case, when the stock is at $78, you could buy the $80 call and buy the $80 put. Or, you could buy the $75 call and the $75 put. That would be a pure Straddle, using the same strike price for both the call and the put.

Here is the point: The stock has to move big time one way or the other. To be profitable on the pure Straddle play, you would have to make enough on the move to get out of one side of the position, either the call or the put to cover the cost of both options and make a profit. Obviously, in real life, you don't have to get out of both calls and puts at the same time. You could leg out of them. For example, if the stock rises, you could get out of the call with a profit, and hopefully enough of a profit to cover the cost of both of the options. Then you could hang on, and end up selling the puts even for 50¢ or $1 and you could pick up whatever cash you can. Even if the stock goes up a bit, it may go down after the earnings because the news is played out. In a pure Straddle play, you would get in at the same time and you would get out at the same time.

A variation of a Straddle is a Strangle. For example, if the stock were at $78, you would buy the $75 put and buy the $80 call. In this case, you are paying less money for the whole position because you are buying each one of these options out-of-the-money. The put is out-of-the-money and the call is out-of-the-money. If you really want to play further out, you could even do the next month and/or the same month and do the $70 puts and the $85 calls. With this example, you would be paying a lot less money, but again, you need time for the option to work.

Remember, time becomes your enemy and you need a big move either way if you do way out-of-the-money calls and way out-of-the-money puts. However, we are going to be doing quite a few of these as we get towards the end of March and the first part of April.

One last point. If you really feel that the stock is going to rise, say it is on a dip and has found support levels and many other factors enter into the picture, including the marketplace in general, the Fed announcement, etc., you would be foolish to play the puts. You would just play the calls. However, if you think earnings are not going to come in on target, many other stocks in that sector are going down, etc., then you would be foolish to buy the calls. The point is, play your hunches with the best information you have. If you flat out 'do not know' which way the stock is going to go, but you know it is going to go one way or the other, that is when you play the pure Straddle and buy *both* positions.

Note: Many of these plays are within one month. You get your best movements on the shorter term options. If you're patient, you might make money or at least break even on both sides of the trade. The only way you'll lose is if the stock doesn't move.

WRITING COVERED CALLS

The process of selling call options against a stock position is still one of my favorite strategies. It's a workhorse. Stock prices are definitely affected by these quarterly movements. Tracking these movements should help you do better at the following:

A. Stock Purchase

Knowing the low points by date will help you purchase stocks at a better time. Either sell the calls immediately or wait until the options are more valuable. Remember, you're selling the upside potential of the stock, so try to get paid well.

B. Choose Better Stocks

You have to choose either high premiums, or lower, yet safer premiums. With high-flying stocks you can get more premium but the risks are greater.

On the riskier stocks, consider selling deeper in-the-money calls. For example: Say a stock has run up to $90. It looks like it's going higher, but it's on a recent high. It has good support at $80. Maybe the $80 calls are the best ones to sell. If the stock backs off you have pre-captured the larger premium (the in-the-money portion of $10, plus the time value). You will still get called out at $80. If you do not necessarily want to sell the stock then consider taking in less option premium by selling the $85 or $90 calls. Remember, the question to ask in determining which strike price to sell: "Do I want to get called out or not?" In this case, we wanted to get called out, plus we were afraid of the stock price backing off.

C. Consider The LOCC™ System (*Wall Street Money Machine, Volume 5: How to Get the Market to Pay for Your Stocks–FREE!*)

This system dictates that you sell farther out options, four to six months. The stock then will move through two, possibly three RLGL periods. You have less cash tied up and more time for a dipping stock to recover.

D. Write Covered Calls in Your IRA

Remember, you can write Covered Calls in your IRA or other pension entity.

Note: On all option-type trades in your IRA/Pension accounts, you will find a huge discrepancy in what you *can* do and what your stock broker *thinks* you can do, or will allow you to do. Have him or her check out www.cboe.com. This web site will make most broker's statements seem foolish. It will definitely end a lot of arguments.

BIG RUN-UPS – FLUFFY PREMIUMS

Putting these different trades aside, let's focus on the sell/buyback strategy in a single scenario. The stock has had a big run-up and it has stalled. You feel this new high price cannot be sustained.

X marks the spot. I had to stop here. It was 6:20AM on March 7, 2001 and I was waiting for someone with a key to come open up the building where we play basketball. He came, and we played for an hour or so. When I was back in the car, I got my broker on the phone. It was the week before expiration and I was cleaning house–going through my accounts and primarily selling calls against stock positions for the month of March.

We checked out Broadcom and did a trade that reminded me of the comment I wrote in the first paragraph, hence, the X marks the spot; but this time "see Spot run," downhill. Broadcom had bottomed

BROADCOM

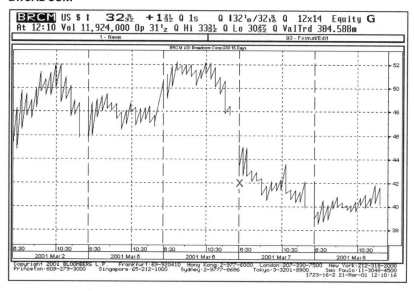

out, or so I thought. It had retreated to the $40s and dipped into the high $30 price range. It was around $50 the week prior when the whole market did a downward spiral. I had every thought that the market, and particularly Broadcom, would start back up. I wrote a covered call at the same time I purchased the stock. I didn't necessarily want to sell the stock, as I think many of these stock prices will rise nicely, especially into this next green light period. (Read that green light period as mid-March through mid- to late-April.)

I had a difficult time choosing the strike price. If I chose the $45 or $50 strike, I'd probably get called out. The $55 and $60 were less money, but then I would take less now, with an extra $5 or $10 if the stock went up to $55 or $60 and held through the expiration date. I owned 400 shares.

I chose the $60 strike price. I sold the option for $1.375, or $137.50 times 4 contracts, for the 400 shares. That's $550. Then, after basketball, the stock was around $44. These same $60 calls were now $0.25 x $0.375. I could buy them back for $0.375, or $37.50 times four, totaling $150. Okay. I've now profited $400 ($550 minus $150) and I still own the stock. The $50 calls were now $1.50 x $1.85. I sold them for $1.50 and took in another $600.

Why the $50 call? Well, let's think it through. My premise was to hold this stock to, and halfway through, the next major move, which I define as the next green light period. However, even though the market has been on a nice rise the last few days, Broadcom, in particular, has gone the opposite way.

Here's an intra-day chart of the NASDAQ for just a few days at the beginning of March, 2001:

Look at Broadcom during this same period:

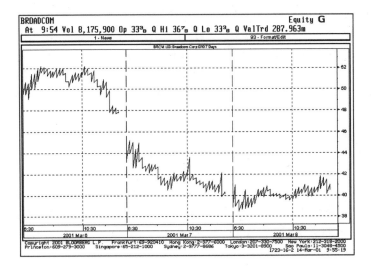

Why the downturn? Broadcom, like so many companies, is conditioned to say all the bad things about themselves. They are all in a rut. It has become fashionable to "good-mouth" and "bad-mouth" your company at the same time.

Back to the $50 call. I wanted to pick up more cash, but I did not want to sell the stock. Let's now look at the potential results:

I purchased Broadcom for $50. I sold the $60 calls for March, bought them back on a dip, and freed up the stock. I then sold the $50 calls. I've taken in $550 ($60 calls) and $600 ($50 calls), or $1,150. I've spent $150 for the middle buy back. I've made $1,000. If the stock rallies and I get called out at $50, that $1,000 is about all I'm going to make. I bought the stock at $50 and sold it at $50.

If the stock doesn't rally, I still keep the $1,000, and own the stock. If it dips again, I could buy back the $50 calls and sell the $45 calls or even the $40 calls. I'm trying to make the point that even in a down drafting market or in a dipping stock, you can still generate income.

Let's say now the stock rises to $50 and is heading higher. The $50 call is just 25¢, right at expiration the stock is at $50.10. Notice how I've switched to pennies, as all the different exchanges are changing from fractions to pennies, even as I write this. If you think the stock is going higher, you could again do a buyback. Spend 25¢, or $100 (remember, we have 400 shares), and free up the stock. You could sell the April $50 calls for $3, or $1,200, or the $55 calls for $1.50 or $600. You're still in the game. If you think it has a near-term peak and might back off, sell the $50s. As the stock dips below $50, you could buy it back again for say $1, or $400. You've pocketed $800 and are ready for the next move.

RLGL Bull Call Spreads

A bull call spread is a variation of covered call writing. Instead of using ownership of a stock for your covered portion of the trade, you use another call position for your covered portion.

Remember our $92 put? Let's use the same example: This time, let's buy the $85 call for $9, or $9,000 and sell the $90 call for $5 or

$5,000. This position costs us a net debit of $4,000. With $4,000 as our cost and our risk, we'll make a profit of $1,000 if everything works. To make maximum profits the stock must stay above $90. You need to get called out.

Let's see what happens. If the stock stays above $90, we will get exercised on. We'll get called out. This time, though, we don't own the stock. We own the right to buy the stock. So we exercise our right to buy the stock at $85 (using SDS, or Same Day Substitution). We make the $5,000, just as if we had purchased the stock for $85,000 and sold the same stock for $90,000, but we do it all with options. We don't net $5,000, as it cost us $4,000 to put this spread in place. That's $1,000 profit (minus commissions).

If the stock drops below $90 we won't get called out. We might be able to sell the $85 call and make a little. If the stock drops below $85 we lose $4,000. In Bullish strategies, you want the stock to go up, or at least stay up above the obligation (strike price), in this case, the $90 strike price. See *Wall Street Money Machine Volume 4: Safety 1st Investing,* for more on this subject.

WRITE, THEN BUY BACK

Here's an interesting Red Light, Green Light covered call play. Let me set this up by stating a certain style of trading many of my students are employing and enjoying: it's sort of a rolling stock covered call in reverse. Here's the set up. What we've taught for years is to buy a stock on dips and sell the call against the stock position on a rise in the stock price. For example: Buy a stock at $16 on a dip; wait for a rise to $18 and sell the $20 calls for say, $1. Then, if the stock continues to rise and you get called out at $20, you make $4 capital gains and keep the $1 option premium. Okay, that's a normal covered call trade.

Here's a twist: Sell the $17.50 call instead. You give up the upside – everything over $18. Actually, you give up everything over $17.50, but you've captured the amount between $17.50 and $18 as the 50¢ will be part of the call premium. The $17.50 call premium is $2 – 50¢ in the money and $1.50 of time value. When you have sold the call, the stock will go up, go down, or stay about the same. Let's explore the moves:

Up: You keep the $2, which, on 1,000 shares of stock, would be $2,000. You get called out at $17.50 and make $1.50 capital gain, or $1,500. Total profit: $3,500.

Down: You keep the $2, or $2,000, then the stock dips to anything over $17.50 and you still sell the stock – you get called out at $17.50. If the stock dips to $17, you keep the stock, you keep the $2,000, and you're ready to do it again next month. We'll get back to this in a moment.

Same: If the stock stays at $18 or so, expiration will come and go. Your stock will be bought away from you at $17.50. But you don't have to let this happen. Remember, you sold the option premium, which included a fair amount of time premium – in this case, $1.50 of the $2. At expiration date, you could buy back ten contracts of this $17.50 strike price calls and end the position. You sold a call giving someone the right to buy 1,000 shares of stock from you, but now have closed out that obligation you created for 60¢, $600 for the ten contracts. You sold the $17.50 calls for $2,000 and now have spent $600 to buy back the position, pocketing $1,400 profit and yes, you still own the stock. You could sell the $17.50 calls again, or the $20 calls for the next month out.

Up/Same: If the stock has stayed the same or gone up, you don't have to wait until expiration to make a move. Let's say the stock moved up to $18.50, and there are still two and a half weeks to expiration. You think the stock is going to fly. The $17.50 calls are now $1.50. Why not more? Because time has elapsed. Yes, the stock has gone up, but time has gone away. The $20 calls are now $1.25. You could buy back the $17.50 calls and simultaneously, or even after a few more days (of increases hopefully), sell the $20 calls. You make more on the calls and a lot more on the stock being sold for $20 instead of $17.50.

Down/Same: We're to the point of explaining the reverse covered call. If the stock dips, buy back the $17.50 call, wait for the next rise, sell the same call again, and on the next dip buy it back again. You might be able to do this two to three times in one month. I've never heard of anyone doing this reverse roll play more than three times before any one expiration date.

Did you catch the dynamics of this style of trade? You're selling calls, first of all. You have a two in three chance of making money – possibly a three in three chance as the call premium will offset the price of a declining stock. Second: you're selling the fluffy time premiums, not buying them. Third: as the stock dips, obviously some time has lapsed. You're buying back the option made cheaper two ways:

1. A decrease in the value of the stock (unless a change in implied volatility kicks it up).

2. A lapse in time. You're doing rolling options, but in reverse.

Just think how much better you'll play these up and down turns as the stocks move into a Green Light period and out of a Red Light period – or vice versa. Use the stock's own patterns, anticipate the news, ride the whole market, and seriously enhance each trade.

6

More
Red Light, Green Light
Cash Flow Strategies

This chapter is a continuation of the explanations of the usage and timing of various trading formulas as we come up on, enter, and leave the "news/no-news" period of time. My attempt is to help you connect the dots. Yes, you know how to start a car, but if you tweak the carburetor a little you could turbo-charge your "wheels" and get where you're going faster – and have more fun on the trip.

Keep enhancing your powers of observation. Included in this chapter are the following strategies:

1. ☑	Blue Chip	9. ☐	Rolling Options
2. ☐	Rolling Stock	10. ☑	Bargain Hunting/Turnarounds
3. ☐	Options	11. ☐	Range Riders
4. ☐	Writing Covered Calls	12. ☑	IPOs
5. ☐	Stock Splits	13. ☐	Spin-offs
6. ☑	Selling Puts	14. ☑	Updates
7. ☐	Bull Call Spreads	15. ☐	Other: Straddles
8. ☑	Bull Put Spreads		

Note: Turnarounds, spin-offs and any other strategies are also mentioned herein. My comments about these extra strategies correspond to comments made in the previous reports about Red Light, Green Light trading in general.

BARGAIN HUNTING

How are our attempts at buying seriously undervalued or hard-hit stocks during the different red light-green light or no-news times?

Downdrafts and Updrafts. We're looking to play either one. When a stock is hit hard, and yet trying to make a comeback, news drives the stock to its extremes. At these times, bargain basement stocks are as sensitive as they can be.

If you have ever heard yourself say, "Well, it can't go much lower," then watch out. $90 to $6 in less than a year, and everyone thinks it's bottomed out as it bounces back to $7, but then...yep, you guessed it, it goes down to $3 (another 50% of its $6 value).

Opportunities abound, but be careful. Don't neglect to check other stocks in the same or related sectors. Check the quarterly news timing and for Pete's sake, know it will be a long time before it's back to $90. There will be many "range rider" type of opportunities along the climb back up.

I chose these three stocks (CMGI, SFE, and ICGE) for this example because they are all incubator type companies. In other words, they take companies public. They own stock in some private companies still waiting to go public. They carry the stock of these companies on their books for a long while. Some have a tremendous book value. You could be buying assets at a discount. That's my true approach to bargain hunting: getting at undervalued assets.

CMGI INC.

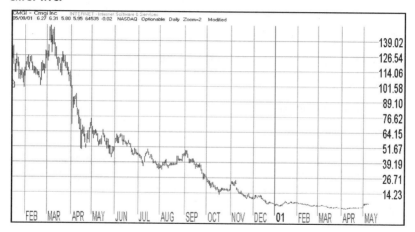

SAFEGUARD SCIENTIFIC

INTERNET CAPITAL GROUP

Look at the three charts (RMBS, MU and JDSU) on these pages. Notice the huge downdraft, and where they are even one year later:

RAMBUS INC.

MICRON TECHNOLOGY

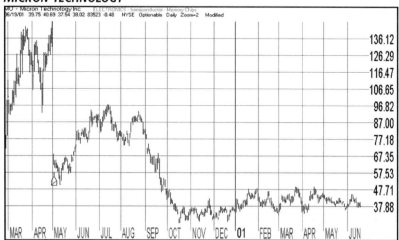

JDS Uniphase

We want to buy stocks that have the highest likelihood of a quick recovery. They're tough to spot. Don't have too much money tied up in any one position. When in doubt, follow earnings. Find out why it's down and see if the company's problems are not only correctable, but are actually being corrected. Consider the following:

A. New management is wonderful news. Many people bet on the jockey, not the horse. I, for one, agree, but news of new management has a short (two weeks to two months) news value. Investors want results and sometimes results take years. The stock gets trashed in the mean time. Watch out.

B. Learn to read the Company's Quarterly Filing statements. Look at earnings. Debt. Book value. Read several to get a feel for how they are written.

C. Many bargain basement stocks have no current earnings. Technical factors drive the stock up and down.

D. Many hard hit stocks form rolling patterns at their support levels. Just when you think your $3 stock hits $5 and is ready to zoom ahead, it backs off to $3 again. It might do this several times in the next six to twelve months.

E. Many of these stocks never recover. If you read the company's management discussion (see B above) and other financial statements in its 10Q or 10K filings, you could have picked up on these tell-tale signs of negative movements.

F. Read shareholder proxy statements in advance of shareholder meetings. There's usually a lot of meat in the written word and between the lines.

Everything is important. Don't minimize any news: the individual storyline of the company and everything else going on in the market place at large. Add to this the news timing and you should be able to make better decisions.

IPOs (INITIAL PUBLIC OFFERINGS)

Initial Public Offerings are not normally affected by a quarterly news cycle. However, they are very much affected by the red or green of the overall marketplace. If stocks are hammered and the whole market is weighed down, many IPO promoters hold back their public announcements.

This is even more true when a whole sector is getting beaten up and the target stock is in that particular class of companies. Conversely, many bad investments are made when things are green – everything is turning to gold, and promoters are rushing companies to market – the good with the bad.

Almost converse to the lack of quality of a company's business plan and prospects for profit, is the incredible quality of the PR campaign behind the stock issuance. Do you think somebody knows something? And more importantly, do you think we're the last to know?

If you follow my IPO approach, which is to ignore the opening hoopla, and either get in before the company goes public or at the 25-day mark – when the 25-day IPO rule kicks in. This 25-days is a quiet period. Once the 25-days are over, the company can do all sorts of things to support the stock: analysts reports, pricing predictions, news releases. Often the stock within this 25-days, after the initial pop-up in price, has fallen back too close to the initial price. If the underwriters are well-known and the company has a great business plan, there will be a tendency for the stock to rise soon after the end of the hush period. It's not uncommon to see a 10-25% rise in the stock price within a few days to a few weeks after the 25-day quiet period has ended.

Look at these charts. I've put a random selection of nine stock charts here. Notice the spike up at the IPO date, then a backing off, then the rise at the end of the 25 day quiet period.

BROADCOM

CACHEFLOW, INCORPORATED

INTERSIL HOLDING CORP.

JUNIPER NETWORKS

KRISPY KREME

OPEN WAVE

PALM INCORPORATED

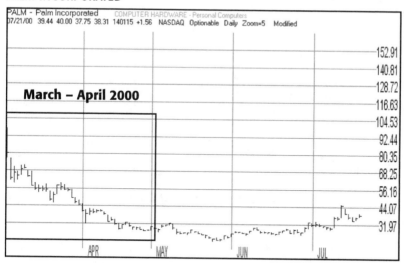

RAMBUS INC.

AVANEX CORPORATION

Check RLGL timing. It's difficult to fight market trends. Don't try to catch a falling piano, as the old saying goes. Play the market at hand.

RLGL SELLING PUTS

First, you must know my affinity for selling options – both calls and puts. Selling puts is a cash flow strategy which, if you're going to use options anyway, stacks the deck in your favor.

Here's the issue; a stock is going up, down, or sideways. When you buy an option, say a put, the price you pay is based on a model – in short, what an option market maker or seller thinks he/she can get for selling it. This model is made up of four things:

1. A risk-free rate of return for comparison purposes,

2. The time left to expiration date,

3. The implied volatility or speculative value, and

4. Any in-the-money portion of the stock price. If the risk is larger, the swings more volatile, the option price will be greater.

When you buy the put, time immediately begins to work against you. If the stock stays the same or goes up, you will lose. You need the stock to go down and down sufficiently in a timely manner for your put, or your right to sell the stock at the strike price to someone else, to go up in value. Example: a stock seems to have peaked at $92. The $90 put for this month is $6 per share. One contract (100 shares) would be $600. Ten contracts would cost $6,000 and you would have the right to sell someone – the "invisible they" – 1,000 shares of this stock. Granted, most people never exercise this right. You buy it at $6, or $6,000 and sell at $9 or $9,000, and make a $3,000 profit, OR you buy for $6,000 and sell for $2,000 and lose $4,000.

Timely. That's the word. If this stock drops to $90, your put might rise to $7. You'd make $1,000. However, if it drops to $90 the Thursday or Friday of expiration day, your $6 put could be worth 25¢. You lose $5.75, or $5,750 (plus commissions).

The other side. The stock drops to $80, almost overnight. There is $10 in-the-money value, plus any time value left to expiration. It could easily be $14. That's $10 in the money plus $4 of time. Sell now for $14,000 and chalk up a nice $8,000 profit.

Let's go the other way. If the stock rises, say to $96 and time elapses, you could lose your whole $6,000, wham, bam, it's gone.

To recap: The stock will go up, down or sideways (stays the same). If you buy a put and the stock goes up, you lose. If the stock stays the same (or goes down slightly), you lose. The stock has to drop pretty significantly for you to win. You have a one in three chance of making money.

Now let's sell the same put. By selling we take on an obligation to let someone sell us the stock at the strike price. We get cash for selling this obligation. You should never sell a put on a stock you do not want to own. If you get a stock put to you, you are buying at wholesale. Using the $6 example on the $92 stock, if we get the stock put to us at $90, our cost basis is $84 ($90 – $6 = $84). Why do we sell for cash and take on this obligation? Answer: to make money. Just because we're willing to buy this stock, we don't necessarily want to! We want to keep all of the $6,000, or most of it.

Here we go. We sell ten contracts for $6,000. We have to have about 20% on hold (margin), that's $18,000. $6,000 cash in and $18,000 on hold if we did ten contracts. Let's see what happens with the "up, down and sideways" in this transaction. If the stock goes up we can just let the option expire and keep the whole $6,000, or we could end the position (obligation) early by buying back the option we sold–hopefully for $1 or $2 – profiting $4,000 or $5,000. If we do this we not only end the obligation, but we stop the margin hold. *One out of three.*

If the stock stays the same, or even goes down a little, we see the position expire and keep the profits. *Two out of three.*

If the stock goes down, we risk having the stock put to us, but we can buy back the position. If the stock goes down, say 50¢ to $1.75, we still won't get it put to us at $90. *Possibly a three in three chance* of making money. I like stacking the deck like this.

If you're worried about taking the stock you should not have done this type of transaction, or you should have converted it into a spread by purchasing the $85 put.

The Red Light, Green Light Effect

Selling puts is like a synthetic stock position. You have all the risks of owning the stock – clear down to a zero downside, but your upside is limited. When you sell something – that's it, your profits are capped off. You can't make more than the $6 or $6,000. Think about it; you have truly put the odds on your side. You know one of three things must happen – up, down, or stay the same.

Because this type of transaction is like a stock position your entrance and exit points should reflect an understanding of the news-no news Periods. When you would buy stock, or buy calls, you could sell puts. It's a cash flow machine. Use all available information to get in and get out at better times. Open positions to generate cash, close positions to capture cash.

The Red Light periods become troublesome for this strategy. As a stock enters a no-news period, the stocks usually leak down. If the stock has gone up and/or stayed up above the strike price, it might be best to spend a little of your profits and end your obligation by buying back the same put you previously sold. Again, the stock can't get put to you with the position closed out. The margin requirement stops. Now, let the stock dip, you don't care. Get ready to sell another put as the stock finds support and heads into the next Green Light period.

RLGL BULL PUT SPREADS

One of my favorite monthly cash flow strategy is still the bull put Spread. This past while it has barely edged out writing covered calls. There are special concerns when doing bull put spreads as you go into a Red Light period, or out of a Green Light period.

A bull put spread is a variation of a pure sell put play. A stock has gone down, but found support at $62. You think it's going up – all indicators point that way. You sell the $60 put for $4.50 or $4,500 if you do ten contracts. You buy the $55 put for $3, or $3,000. You pocket $1.50 or $1,500 as this is a credit spread. It's a $5 spread so you risk $5,000, but $1,500 came from the market, so $3,500 of your own money is at risk and on hold. $3,500 at risk to keep $1,500, if all stays right.

You should not do this strategy unless you're really bullish on the stock. You do have an obligation to take this stock at $60. If the stock stays above $60 everything is fine. The option will expire and you keep the $1,500. If the stock dips below $55, you could lose your $3,500 (SDS or same day substitution kicks in) and though you get put the stock at $60, the other side of the married position is exercised at $55 – you put the stock to someone at $55. You lose $3,500. Note: this is one caution I have for online or Internet trades. It takes a good stock broker to marry up these positions, get the best prices (say with cross market trades), and get you out the right way. I wish online trading hadn't been invented. I spend a large amount of time at my seminars dealing with bad trades. Almost 100% of the time, the horror stories come from online traders. They so desperately want to be independent that they totally forget about the value of teamwork and having true professionals executing their trades.

Let's take a look at a real-life example from my report that was posted on WIN on March 9, 2001. This was at 8:59AM PST:

I checked on Microsoft, which was down about $2.50. My Trading Department has had to relocate due to the earthquake causing damage to part of our building, so I haven't been able to keep real close contact with them. However, it seems to me that Microsoft might rally back into the $60 range. Almost every year in the middle of March there is a little rally in Microsoft that heads into the earnings season. Again, this Red Light, Green Light period takes precedence right now as all the new earnings forecasts come out. I figured a $55/$50 bull put spread would be in order on Microsoft. I put the trade out to sell the $55 puts and buy the $50 puts on a bull put spread for a net credit of 50¢. I don't know if I have been hit on that transaction as of yet, we will let you know if it comes through.

I am also considering, if Microsoft gets down to $56 today or Monday before March 15th or even before expiration date, buying the March $55 calls. Let me give you the prices on those as of a few minutes ago: The $55 calls were $3 x $3.25 and the stock was at $57.1875 at the time I checked on this. The $50 calls for March were 66.25¢ x $7.75, so you would pay $7.75 and the stock is at $57.1875, so $7.1875 of the $7.75 in the money. You are really only paying very little for the time value, which is obviously a short time, just until next week. If Microsoft goes back up to $59, you would almost go tick for tick because it is nearly all intrinsic time value.

I considered that play, but I first want to see if Microsoft, having gone down $2.50, will go down any more today. Again, if it hits $56, I think it has fairly good support at that level and I will jump in at that point in time.

One problem with a dipping stock is if the price (on expiration) is between the spread prices. You could get a stock put to you, but can't exercise the bottom portion. You should monitor these positions wisely and end the position if possible. Also, if you get put the stock, you should consider selling it right away so you don't have too much cash tied up.

RLGL How To Play It

If the stock is on a dip and it looks like a good entrance point, but the stock is heading into a Red Light period, you should consider the following:

1. Wait before you jump in. By waiting, you might see the stock dip to $56 or so. Then, you could do the $55/50 bull put spread, or even the $50/45. More safety.

2. Move down to the $55/50 spread right now. Okay, so you only make $1 ($1,000) instead of $1.50 ($1,500) but you have $5 more of safety. It's like defense in football–extra padding.

3. Consider a bear call spread. A bear call spread is another favorite monthly cash flow spread strategy. It's also a credit spread. You sell the $65 call for say $4 and buy the $70 call for $2.50. Again, you make $1,500 with $3,500 on hold and at risk. Use bear call spreads when you think a stock will go down.

   Note: The whole market has Red Light, Green Light periods, and so do individual stocks. Before you play stocks, know when their quarter ends, when their Board meets – nothing happens until the Board members meet, and understand the effect of other stocks in the same sector.

4. Beware of what the whole market place is doing.

   Again, your particular stock's Red Light and Green Light period may be different than the whole market place. The company may have an off year-end, therefore off-calendar quarters. I have observed that, even though the company has an odd quarter-end, its stock price can be affected by other news, say the market in general. It can move in sympathy with the sector it's in, or move along with other stocks as the Fed raises or lowers the discount rate. Some stocks are so big, so widely traded (like Dell and Pfizer) that, even though they have odd year-ends, their announcements and pre-announcements might affect other stocks which are in a normal red light calendar period.

BUCS — WIDE ANGLE

We could do the same type of play as a reverse covered call by buying a call option on the stock and selling another call option at a higher strike price.

Example: A stock is rolling between $40 and $60. Buy the $30 calls when the stock is at $44, out two to three months (you need to give this time), for $16. Sell the $50 calls for $5. Spend $16,000, take in $5,000, and have tied up $11,000. If the stock goes to $50 or above, you get called out. You make $20,000 – minus the $11,000 it cost to put this trade (married position) in place. That's $9,000 before commissions.

Okay, now the buyback. As time elapses, the price of the $50 call will deteriorate the fastest. The $30 call is mostly intrinsic value anyway. On a pull back, buy back the $50 calls for $2, and then on the next rise sell it again for $2, or this time sell the $45 call for $4, pocketing another $4,000.

The news periods here have the same effect as other bullish strategies. You weigh out support levels, dips and peaks, news announcements, and what the whole market place is doing. All of these factors are important. If even one factor is out of place, do not do the deal – look elsewhere.

Bull call spreads are best suited for up markets. Most up markets need good news to happen. Do bull call spreads as we're heading into a good, green light period.

Note: I do these types of spreads in the money. For example, if we do the $90/95 bull call spread, the stock would have to climb above and stay above $95 for the transaction to work perfectly.

RLGL BLUE CHIP INVESTING

I love owning great stocks. I especially love it when I can buy those stocks at discount prices. I also like selling from time to time, when the stock I own is on a tear and peaks out. If I honestly feel the high price cannot be maintained, say after a 20% increase in three weeks, then I'll sell.

Blue chip portfolios are wonderful for writing covered calls. If I don't want to necessarily sell the stock, I'll sell the call on a nice price increase in the stock, or farther out of the money so I won't get called out.

I also sell puts on nice stocks. If I do get them put to me, I buy them at a wholesale price. If the stock rises in price I just keep the put premium.

I have rarely regretted selling a stock at the peak of the Green Light period and then buying the same stock $5 to $15 cheaper in the next Red Light period.

One other viewpoint is, when stocks are on major lows after a retracement of their upward spiral, these stocks can be purchased as cheaply as a call option cost just a few months before. For example, at the time of this writing, Lucent (LU) had tanked to $6 or so. Look at the chart:

LUCENT

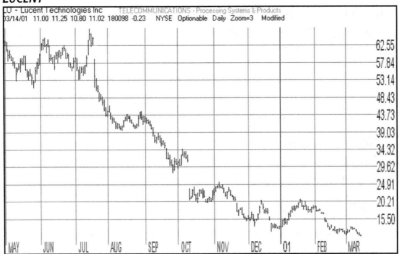

Several months ago, when the stock was at $60, the $60 (LEAPS®), expiring in about two years, were $14. Think of it. These LEAPS® expire. They pay no dividends. The stock, for $6, seemed like a bargain. And, if you choose, the stock can be purchased on margin. You would only have $3, or $3,000 of your own cash tied up, to own 1,000 shares of stock; instead of ten contracts, of the stock options.

RLGL ALL OTHER STRATEGIES

I could divide out turnarounds, spin-offs and other strategies, but my comments about the strategies previous to this section will hold.

Each strategy has a beginning, a middle and an end. Know your exit and then be prepared to get out and cut your losses if the trade doesn't work as planned.

Use the market at hand and the news time period to put your money in the way of movements, or out of the way of hurtful moves. The market, and each stock, are in continuous flux – some slow, some fast. Watch and learn. Connect the dots. Notice patterns. Practice and then practice some more. Learn from your mistakes. And remember, "the biggest fish you'll ever catch is still swimming in the ocean."

7

COMPELLING REASONS

Momentum. Position Trading. OMFs (Other Motivating Factors). Stock Splits. Earnings Reports. Share buy backs. Red Light, Green Light periods.

As I instruct people to get their money in the way of movements, I've frequently camped awhile on the notion that a stock moves for a reason. I've asked my students in seminars to write down in big bold letters – *What compelling reason does this stock have to go up (or down)?*

If you are playing a stock for a two to three day trade, and you want it to go from $62 to $66 and then plan to get out of the option at that point, you should be doing so for a reason. If it's just hopeful thinking, you'll probably be disappointed more times than you like. If it's because it's a few days before earnings are to be out, and whisper numbers are looking good, or it's bounced off of a support level, and rumors are that the company's management is to announce a stock split, chances are it will move upward.

First, check the surrounding news. Are there other bad earnings forecasts? Is the whole marketplace on an uptrend or a downtrend? Ask yourself, what can go wrong? What can stop or hinder this up movement?

Here's the point: If there is no compelling reason for the stock to move, you should stay clear. Remember, no news is death to these stocks. Bad news has a tremendous downward pull. Even good news, if it's tempered with negative forecasts, can spell defeat for this trade.

Remember, remember, remember – current stock prices, and price movements, are based on the *anticipation of future earnings.*

With the stock market being as topsy-turvy as it currently is, I am constantly looking for specific trades that have momentum – either up or down. These are trades that have what I would call a "compelling reason" or what I call the impending event. One of those trades right now would be to play companies that are rallying into a split. The second trade would be to buy put options on the stock at the split time. Fundamental analysis and technical analysis are designed to measure ways to justify stock prices and to determine which way prices are heading.

In the open air marketplace, today's stock price reflects all kinds of information made available and the anticipation of future earnings. This is why you may see such a high concentration of attention on what the Federal Reserve is going to say. In short, if the Fed is going to raise the interest rate, and in nine to twelve months corporate earnings will go down because of the high cost of borrowing money, and there will not be much in profit and earnings, the stock price will come down now. The stock market reacts today based on what a company will be earning in nine months or twelve months or even in the next one and a half years.

Let's take a brief look at three ways to analyze or look at stocks. Then, we'll take a look at options and see the connection.

FUNDAMENTALS

One way to look at the value of stock is to take a "fundamental approach." The "fundamentals" system primarily looks at the earnings of a company. This is often stated as a P/E, or price to earnings ratio. Simply put, the P/E states how much each dollar of earnings will cost you. A P/E of 32 means you will pay $32 to get at $1 of earnings. For a clearer view of P/E, let's look at some selected excerpts from *Wall Street Money Machine, Volume 5*:

One caution: when you get the P/E you don't necessarily know if it's past tense, or "trailing earnings;" or if it's future tense, or "projected earnings," or if it's a blend of both. Projected earnings are someone's guess at what the company will earn over the next year. The projected earnings are usually higher than what happened last year so the P/E will be lower. You see, a lot of people like low P/Es. You are buying the future earnings if you buy the stock today, but it's also more honest to look at what the company has done in the past. A blended P/E would give us the best of both worlds. I like it best when the company – or a news article – bases their P/E on six months back and six months forward. It is a better reflection of where the company really stands.

I believe earnings are a key to stock movements. I've shouted it from the rooftops. Follow earnings, follow earnings. Is the company profitable? Are they (and the earnings) expanding or contracting? Are their sales growing? What are they doing with their money? Are earnings growing because they've acquired another company? Will this acquisition slow them down? Are earnings growing from cost cuttings (sometimes good, or can contraction be bad?). Learn everything you can about a company's earnings.

TECHNICAL VIEWPOINTS

Technical analysis uses numbers to help us determine movements. These technical measurements help show when a stock will turn up, or go higher, and when a stock will decline, die or turn around. This study uses moving averages to show when a stock gets in a buy or sell range. Other technical viewpoints use call and put volume increases. Some technical analysts like gaps, when a stock price gaps up or down to show the direction it will go thereafter. Others use money flows to see if money is entering the stock or leaving. There are many more, including some way-out planetary models. A fun technical is when the NFC or AFC wins the Super Bowl. The market goes up or down, they say.

Many people, like me, are busy. I know of these measuring sticks and I have three good stockbrokers who love the technical aspects of all this. I listen and use their advice sometimes. I'll say, "I want to buy 200 shares of Microsoft." They'll say, "Wait one or two days, it should drop a dollar or two." I question and get an ear full. I wait. They are often right. But Microsoft at $67 instead of $64 is not a big difference if it does a split and you sell 400 shares at $50 a few months later. That's a $6,600 profit. At $64 I would have made an extra $600. Like I said, not a big deal, sometimes.

Now, when it comes to option trading – especially quick turn trades – every dollar is important. Technical analysis tells us when to get in and when to get out. Let's spell it "technEEcal" analysis. The "EE" are for Entrance and Exit points.

OTHER MOTIVATING FACTORS

Now the fun begins. Once we start to use fundamental aspects and technical entrance and exit points, then we realize that newsy items or other motivating factors also drive the stock or option. Earnings reports drive stocks up and down. So does the anticipation of good or bad news. Watch for patterns. Look for good buying opportunities.

Spin-offs and IPOs are news events. (See Chapter 6, More Red Light, Green Light Cash Flow Strategies, for more information about how to trade on these.) So are mergers, takeovers, and stock splits. Lawsuits – either instituted or ended – play into the picture, as does a management change.

One other major factor in the Red Light, Green Light movements, are the positive or negative movements of the whole marketplace. If we see a flat market like 1994, or a boom market like 1996-1998, or even a disastrous market like the year 2000, it's almost as if all contrary news has only a minimal impact. The company has great news, but the marketplace is going down. Your stock's good news (a squirt gun) is drowned by the torrent of negative news (a fire hydrant) on the news wires every day.

Some thoughts:

1. If the market is on a tear and momentum players are everywhere, and it gets to the point that otherwise "non-stock market" people

are pouring their money into the market, it seems that negative warnings from companies are sloughed off. Seriously, we saw companies in 1998 and 1999 not making money – saying that they were not now and that they would not in the future make any money. People were paying 2000 times earnings for their stock. They were second mortgaging their houses to get the money to do so. It was ridiculous. The news and the warnings existed, people just forgot logic and propriety and jumped in.

2. On the other side are companies with decent earnings, nice growth, but in a year like 2000, all the good news couldn't outweigh the continuous stream of negativity. Actually, I thought there would have to be a correction all along. One of my rules is this: "Everything Returns to the Norm."

    Yes, there was a flight to quality during these times but even the quality stocks got caught in the downdraft. Remember the old market maxim: "Don't try to catch a falling piano." It was sure true in 2000 and throughout 2001.

It's time for a time out. At the end of the Vietnam war, I found myself in the Air Force as a Chinese linguist. The classroom study areas were being taken over by new Vietnamese language trainees. Seriously, the German, Chinese, Russian, Korean, etc., students were being pushed out for more Vietnamese students. These Vietnamese language study programs took over whole buildings. I kept thinking, "But the war is over. It's been over for two years, and they're still coming." A peacetime military machine is difficult to maintain at peak efficiency levels. You see, they scheduled needs, in this case thousands of linguists, up to two years or more in advance. It was hard to stop the flow. We were in California shouting to the East Coast, "Hey you guys, the war is over!"

Now, you have to be wondering what this has to do with the Red Light, Green Light, news/no-news periods? There is a connection here. In my Red Light, Green Light seminar (now wonderfully reproduced in a Home Study Course), I mention how many company bigwigs have fallen into a reporting rut.

Here's how it has played out. Stocks shot up. They entered never never land. Even the company's boards, management and others knew their stocks were too high for their current earnings. You heard analysts (trying to justify their recommendation) saying things like this: "The stock at $260 is not bad, based on earnings projected in three to five years."

I'm sure they didn't want their stocks to tank, but they did want a reprieve – or at least an end to the wild run-up. Politicians got involved. Other government officials weighed in. Remember, "Irrational exuberance?" These new players set the tone and again, like lemmings, corporate heavyweights read from the new script.

Virtually every day, but especially in the pre-earnings season and as their SEC documents were filed, press releases, news conferences, interviews flew out the door – with a twist. "Oh, we're earning money (then under their breath – "hundreds of millions more than before…") but we see a slowdown in revenues, sales, growth, etc. Again the driving sentence: Current stock prices are based on the anticipation of future earnings.

Left and right – companies beating their estimates, making untold millions, had stocks dipping $2 to $22 overnight.

Now, it's time for a new rut. Yes, honesty is the best policy, but they don't need to overplay the negative. Those remarks have been tucked away in their filings, that is where they should stay. They need to honestly state their direction, profit potential, future earnings – in less harsh terms. It's time for a change. It's been two years and more Vietnamese language students are coming. Enough already.

3. The streets of San Francisco must be one of the best places for car chase scenes. The views are beautiful as the cars go up, and then shoot up, literally flying through the air at the top of hills. Then the downward chase, hitting everything in sight, spinning around corners, and then, yep, back up with another airborne police car chasing them.

    This, I feel, is a good depiction of the stock market of late – at least of many stocks in the hi-chase (tech) arena.

They shoot up the hill like a man shot out of a cannon, but then gravity takes over. Airborne, there is no where to go but down. Their stock prices cannot be sustained. They're not only airborne, but the air is mighty thin. Their flight is brief. Airsickness sets in.

The lead car and all the others in the chase pack come crashing back to earth. That would be okay, but the earth right there is not flat. It's downhill. These cars need good brakes, or even parachutes – but most crash into other barriers. Many things go down with them. Carnage.

The car is the stock price. The hill up or down is the marketplace. The marketplace can hinder or help the movement, but after all the hype and hoopla, these two, the car and the hill, blend to become one with the universe.

I try to point out these things in my constant talks at my seminars. Watch out! It's all hype! Check earnings. Lately, I've felt like Chicken Little. The sky is not really falling, I know, but stock prices are. Learn from it. Get better at using effective measuring sticks. Don't fight gravity or any other natural financial laws. If you do, you'll be moo goo gai pan in a San Francisco Restaurant.

This current "rut" will change as two things happen:

1. Corporate leaders quit bad mouthing their future.

2. Everyone quits their 25% to 50%, year over year, earnings growth rate expectations. The party was good while it lasted, but as of the beginning of 2001, we need to get back to the norm. 4% to 10% revenue growth and slightly higher earnings growth are historically feasible. Hold management to these reasonable growth expectation levels and stock prices will be easier to measure and more stable.

COMPELLING REASONS

Listed below are news events which would constitute a compelling reason for a stock to move up or down.

1. A stock being added to the S&P 500, or DJIA 30; other major indices, or groupings of stocks held in trusts (Spiders, like QQQ, SPY, MDY, DIA, FFF, etc.). Why? Because many funds buy all the stocks in an index. They are widely followed and widely owned.

2. A stock being taken off one of the lists mentioned in #1. Stocks like this trend down, unless there is other good news. Why? Some funds and other trusts must sell these stocks. Note: not all stocks which discontinue trading in an index are officially dropped. Some merge with other companies, moving, for example, the S&P 500 to 499 companies. They need a new entry.

3. Mergers. In many stock swap deals, there is a period of arbitrage. There is a ratio merger; say two shares of X for one share of Y. At the time of the actual merger, the price/ratios will be in line, but at the announcement and until the actual merger, there could be a discrepancy and a chance to buy the stock or option on the stock which you think will move the most. Each situation is so different that you need to get the details and put a pencil to it. We put as much as we can on W.I.N. at www.wadecook.com. Mergers with a lot of expensive new debt will have a tough time. Excessive debt is a killer of business.

4. Share buy backs are good if the company actually goes through with the purchase. Many programs end with unpurchased stocks. Some stall as the current price of the stock has risen above their purchase price authorization. A share buy back can add strength to other good news – especially a profitable, well-run company.

5. Spin-offs. I like spin-offs. This is where a company spins off a subsidiary company, or a division. If the parent company is raising cash (through an IPO spin off) it could bode well. This news is usually brief. Soon, the baby company has to make it on its own.

6. Lawsuits. Starting lawsuits is a bummer. Ending lawsuits is seen as good. The news is brief. It plays out fast. Remember the media have to get out new editions tomorrow.

7. Seasonal events and weather: hotels, cruise lines, airlines in summer; fuel, clothing, Christmas shopping in winter.

8. Catastrophes, like a Presidential assassination, an earthquake, a nuclear accident, or a Terrorist attack can be played up or down; insurance companies, energy companies, etc.

9. Government news: mergers, buyouts, enterprise zones, government tax increases or reductions, lawsuits, etc., all add to the mix.

10. Government Agency News: Crop reports, housing starts, CPI (Consumer Price Index), PPI (Producer Price Index), and a host of other reports. Note: you may see moves just as big in anticipation of these reports as you do after the actual report is given. Remember: Buy on rumor, sell on fact.

11. January Effect. There is a flight of money in January to the stocks with the most potential. January is usually an up month. The move into equity starts in mid-December. I call it the year-end rally. Why? Many big funds want to own great stocks for window dressing and get their money in the way of January in-flows of money.

You see in January, there are millions of dollars once again pouring into 401K, IRAs, pensions, new budgets, etc. The pension money deposits peter out in July and August as many people hit their maximum contribution level. For four to five months these funds go on a diet. January is here and the new year brings new money.

Did you catch my statement: They want to get their money into these investments in advance of our, or should I say, "the little guy's" money. They get in. We get in and push the stocks up, and buy at higher prices. They get out. We sit there with our lower-priced stocks, wondering what happened. Where have all the flowers gone?

COMPELLING REASONS – NOT

Let me share with you what are not compelling reasons.

1. Stockbroker recommendations, even though thought-out, are not a reason to drive up a stock. Now, however, if the stock broker knows what you're looking for, has current information on news, support lines, gaps, or a host of other factors which could end up helping you spot movements, then GREAT!

2. Friend's "hot tips." Enough said.

3. Wishful thinking is not a compelling reason. Base your decision on events which can make a serious move. Remember, if you're playing options, the stock has to move and move it must in a timely manner.

4. Weather, catastrophes, earthquakes, etc., are usually events which happen and then the markets rebound before you know it.

5. TV news interviews play out fast. Almost too fast to play. You'd have to be a magician to consistently make money.

COMPELLING REASONS RECAP

Now, let's put this all together with some more timeless wisdom from Wall Street Money Machine, Volume 5:

Fundamentals / Technicals / OMFs

Fundamental Analysis	helps us know	WHAT to buy or sell
Technical Analysis	helps us know	WHEN to buy or sell
OMFs	help us know	WHY (to buy or sell) NOW

That's it. Use all three. Don't ignore any of this. With the use of all three methods, you'll make better and quicker decisions. Your "meter drop™" cash profit potential should take off.

Let me reiterate the statement that I make constantly in my Red Light, Green Light Home Study Course. It is simply this:

1. The stocks move in anticipation of a news event.

2. Stocks move at the news event based on the quality of the news.

3. Stocks also move in tandem with the marketplace in general.

Here is a W.I.N.™ update I did on Krispy Kreme. Please read every line. You'll see converging news events (seven total) dog-piling on this stock in a two to three week period. Then in a few months, you can go back, check the W.I.N. archives and see how well I did.

DAY 1: THURSDAY, MARCH 8, 2001
KRISPY KREME (KKD), W.I.N. UPDATE

Good morning everyone! This is Wade.

We're rocking and rolling here – we're getting our building back in shape again. The earthquake shook us up in more ways than one. I have a lot of different trades I have been doing the last couple of days and I will try to get you up to date on several of them.

With the stock market being as topsy-turvy as it currently is, I am constantly looking for specific trades that have momentum – either up or down. These are trades that have what I would call a "compelling reason" to move one way or the other. One of those trades right now would be to play companies that are rallying into a stock split. The second trade at the time of the actual split, would be to buy put options. You saw me do this a few weeks ago on Southwest Airlines (LUV).

I want to address the situation with Krispy Kreme (KKD). Krispy Kreme came out with earnings last night about 5¢ ahead of estimates. The stock has moved up about $3.50 to around $77 (as of the last few minutes) after closing yesterday around $74.

The other thing coming up on Krispy Kreme is the two-for-one stock split with a pay date of March 19, 2001. That will be two Mondays from now, with the ex-dividend date on the Tuesday right after that. Now I am looking at this stock and thinking, if it were at $71 or $72, I would definitely be playing the rally into the stock split, and I would be hoping for it to go from $72 to $74 or maybe $76-$77. Remember, we don't do the rally into the stock split unless there are certain characteristics that exist, and for this trade right now, they don't exist. I might be wrong on that: the stock might go up to $80-$85 into the stock split, because of a precedent setting $100 plus, a long time ago, but I just don't see it happening here, now that the news is already out.

Now again, we are looking for a "compelling reason," or what we call the impending event. One impending event just happened yesterday with the earnings announcement.

Gather all the information and then do the best job you can at playing your hunches.

I was looking at playing a put option into the March expiration date, thinking there is going to be a downdraft right after the split. I know there are a lot of reasons going against that rationale, so let me tell you about the many different things dog-piling on this one scenario. I would usually play this into a closer time period, say a Thursday – Friday or even the Monday – Tuesday of the day after the stock split, and then I would buy the puts on that last little rally. In this case, however, with the earnings out right now I think the news is played out. Here is what I see dog-piling onto this scenario:

The Federal Reserve announcement scheduled for March 20th. I think right here at the end of this Red Light period, everyone is looking out for good news. I see it everywhere. When all the bears are out there (and it seems even the bulls have turned into bears) that is usually the time a marketplace turns around – and I see that happening right now. People are counting on the almost certainty that the Federal Reserve will lower the discount rate at their March 20th meeting. That should be very bullish on the market, and I think a lot of that anticipation is built in. We have seen the market rebound in the last week from the 10,300 level up to 10,800. Yes, it might push up a little bit more, but I just don't see it going up that much. Maybe it will bump against 10,800 or 10,900 and even 11,000 again, but that will take a lot of work and a lot of good earnings forecasts to make it happen.

The other thing I see happening are these manipulated earnings forecasts. I see several corporate statements that seem to be in the rut of bad-mouthing their own earnings forecasts. I see this trend as a short-term negative but a long-term positive – it says that people will start taking a more rational approach to stock prices in general.

People have come to expect incredible earnings growth over the last few years. I did not say earnings, but earnings growth; like 50% earnings compounded year over year. Earnings at 20% or 25% compounded quarter over quarter. It is almost a fairy tale situation to think that these companies can continue to grow at 25%-50% and even 100% per year. The stocks have become so overly inflated that when they get up into the stratosphere where there is no more oxygen, they just have to come down. You have been hearing me say this for almost two and a half years. It is not just the stock prices that are high, but everybody is gambling on earnings continuing to grow in order to justify these high prices.

Finally, we are starting to see some rationale come back into their statements. People are hoping that the marketplace in general, the analysts, the stockbrokers, the stock buyers, all of the small investors out here will quit expecting 50% compounded growth rates. As we get back to a normal growth rate, say 5% to 10% per year, that in and of itself is a high expectation for a company to maintain. Remember, "Current stock prices are a reflection of the anticipation of future earnings."

Fundamental analysis and technical analysis are designed measuring sticks to justify stock prices and to determine which way prices are heading. But in the open-air marketplace, today's price reflects all kinds of information made available and the anticipation of future earnings. This is why you see such a high concentration of energy on what the Federal Reserve is going to say. In short, if the Fed is going to raise the interest rate, and in nine to twelve months corporate earnings will go down because of the high cost of borrowing money, and there will not be that much in profit and earnings, the stock price might come down. The stock market reacts today based on what a company will be earning in nine months or twelve months or even in the next $1^1/_2$ years. That is a short example of what current stock prices do to reflect earnings in about a year. Now the next sentence I want to say, I use in all my seminars: "Everything returns to the norm." Traditional New York Stock Exchange P/E Ratios are 19.2 or 20 times earnings, and when a New York Stock Exchange company's stock price gets way high or way low, everything will return to the norm. If NASDAQ P/E Ratios are between 40 and 60 times earning and you have companies up in the 200 and 800 times earnings, remember, everything will return to the norm. When you are looking at stock prices, look at your prices compared to the norm, and the norm will always take precedence in the long run. Things will return to the norm. Keep that in your thinking process.

Now back to my point. With the corporate earnings being made today and heading into this next Green Light period, what we are seeing first before the end of March, or March 31st, the calendar quarter, where most companies have a December 31st year end and therefore a March 31st quarter end, you see a tremendous amount of news hitting the street. Not by all companies and not on any certain date, but sometime before the end of the calendar quarter, they will start making earnings forecasts. Remember a few years ago with Qualcomm, Inc. (QCOM). Certain analysts were saying their earnings were going to be $1.30 and Qualcomm officials were saying "Better make it higher." They would come out at $1.50 and they would say "Better make it higher." Then they would come out with analyst reports and say $1.70 and Qualcomm officials said "Better make it higher". Well, sure enough, they came out with incredible earnings about that time, but they could not be sustained.

My point was, a couple of years ago, everybody way coming out with these awesome reports and forecasting higher and higher earnings and the stock prices reflected it. Today, the exact opposite is happening. Almost since Alan Greenspan said the words "Irrational Exuberance" and a few corporate bigwigs like Microsoft's Steve Ballmer, said that these stocks were overpriced, you have seen a total negative trend in almost all earnings reports. Things like, "We have beat our estimates, but we don't see revenues going up in the next quarter or the next year." You hear some negative excuse to keep the stock from racing forward based on some high expectations of future earnings. I think, until the marketplace absorbs all this negative news and the mindset of these corporate earnings forecast changes its tone, we are going to have a tough time in the marketplace. We need to see many people stop saying negative stuff on press releases or on CNBC. Let the entire negative stuff stay in their SEC filings. I think that they almost always overplay it.

Picking up on what I just said, this marketplace – especially the news media – reacts so quickly to news: the anticipation of news, who is going to be on CNBC, the actual earnings reports, etc. Sometimes it is two or three hours and the news is played out. Especially in a weak marketplace and seeing what I hope is the tail end of a bear market for the last year or so. But the point is, news is played out very quickly when it is made public.

One example is this news of Krispy Kreme. I am being told by my stockbroker that Krispy Kreme is in an uptrending pennant and it looks like it wants to break out. Well, that is one technical viewpoint and I have to take that into consideration. We have to take everything into consideration, including the fundamental analysis of the company and the technical analysis.

Let me wax philosophical for just a moment. Remember earlier I said that everything returns to the norm, and I had mentioned the NASDAQ range for P/E ratios. I asked my stockbroker what is the P/E ratio for Krispy Kreme? Remember, this could change every second, but at that time, the stock was just a little bit above $77 and the P/E ratio was 87 times earnings. So what does that tell you? Yes, Krispy Kreme is on an expansion. But can this expansion help this stock keep trading at such a high P/E?

Let me interject a personal note. I feel very sorry for those of you that do not live near a Krispy Kreme doughnut shop. If you have not had a Krispy Kreme, they are simply awesome in all definitions of the word awesome. I personally believe it is worth getting on an airplane and flying to a city that has a Krispy Kreme just to have one. They are that good.

Another consideration in all of this is to remember the Red Light, Green Light period, and we are coming into the end of March which is the start of the anticipation of the news in the next calendar quarter. When I called up and asked about Krispy Kreme, I checked on the year-end. They have a January 31st year-end and are already talking about the 2002 fiscal year. That changes everything. If you remember from my Red Light, Green Light Home Study Course, we talk about companies that have these off calendar quarters and off year-ends. Even though they have an off year-end, many times that has to be taken into account and is important. Sometimes it is almost unimportant as the end of their calendar quarters and their actual filings are also at a time when other companies are giving forecasts-type statements. So you must look at each company individually and put it into perspective.

At the same time, I asked what the P/E ratio was and it was 87 times earnings. Put that into your thinking cap. You are going to make a play or not make a play based on information, and here you have a company that is at $80 and is close to 90 times earnings. If everything returns to the norm, it could go down to 40 times earnings or 60 times earnings. However, Krispy Kreme is on a major up trend because it is still expanding all over the country.

I also would like to play this rally into the stock split and then play a put, but I have a feeling this rally might be played out and I am usually the last to know. If I am going to do a rally into the stock split, I want the stock to have gone up the $77-$80 range in the near term and then have backed off. Maybe after the stock split announcement to the low $70's to the high $60's and then get ready for it to rally back to $76 to $77, which was the near term high. However, in this case, the stock was at $71-$72 when I started looking at it a few weeks ago and it has rallied up to $74-$75 in anticipation of the earnings. Again, I am the last to know.

Who knows about this good earnings announcement coming out? Obviously, the company keeps it hush-hush, but there has to be people that know all kinds of things, from analysts to others following the company. They look at trends and growth. They do a detailed study of the company, and try to figure out what their earnings report is going to be. At the same time, many of the big players try to get their money in the way of movement. So the players will jump into a stock and drive it up in hopes that many of the small investors will follow suit at the $77 range up to $80. Then, they get out. See, their play was to get in at $71 and to get out at $76-$77, while all the news was coming out. We, as the last to know, are getting in when all the big guys are getting out.

I don't know if that is exactly the case in this scenario. I am giving this information in a general way to show you that many of the major funds and other players get their money in the way of movements. They do so by buying the stock or by buying the options, and are out when the rest of us finally find out about it.

So we get caught holding the stock at $77 or $80, when the stock goes back to $75 or $74 and we wonder what happened. What happened to the air in the tires? The momentum is gone and we are stuck with the stock. Many times when making my trades, I say to myself, "I am the last to know" and when I do that, I realize that the play may already be over by the time I think about getting involved.

Now let's review and recap this whole situation.

1. We have a whole marketplace that seems to have gone topsy turvy or bottomed out, and I hope that is a true statement.

2. We have a stock split coming up on March 19th, which is a little over a week away.

3. We have a Federal Reserve announcement coming up.

Krispy Kreme

March 8 - 13

Courtesy of Bloomberg, 2001

4. We have a company that is expanding and growing and has just come out with a pretty good earnings report. The stock went up the day of the earnings announcement, shot higher and backed off slightly in a matter of minutes.

5. We have an off year calendar quarter that has to be taken into the mix.

6. We have an up-trending pennant on the stock.

As for the rest of the marketplace, we are not entering a green light period of time.

Having said all of that, I still must play my hunch. All bodes well for Krispy Kreme, but my feeling is, this play is over. Its year-end is over, its earnings are out, and it did really, really well. The stock has gone up $8-$9 in the last week or so in anticipation of everything, and yes, it is coming up on the split and it might go up to $80 or $82. At that time, I will definitely buy some April $80 or $75 puts.

Again, I checked on the near-term puts. The March $75 puts were going for $1.50 and the April $70 puts were going for $2.875 x $3.25. I went ahead and bought 20 contracts of the March $75 puts at $1.50, I figured I could have $3,000 at risk. Again, this is my risk-cash flow capital, this is not my mainstay money, it is just a small amount I am going to put up in advance of this potential move.

Obviously, I want the stock to go down now so I will make money on the put, but I am also looking for a triple or a double on this play I will take a slight profit or slight loss and be out of the trade. This is designed to be a two or three day trade.

I also purchased a little further out, the April $70 put. If the stock goes through the stock split at $78 or $80, it will go down to 2 shares at $40. I think then it may back off from $40 to $36 to $34 and the $70 puts would become the $35 puts. These puts hopefully will become more valuable between now and April, which is just a little over a month away. I went ahead and bought 10 contracts of the April $70 puts.

The reason I am giving you all of this information is, simply because, when it is all said and done, you have to play your hunches. My stockbroker tried to talk me out of these. He thought the up trending pennant (and he puts a lot of emphasis on the technical aspects on all this), outweighed anything in the negative downdraft. I however, with all this information out there and still more good news, think we are still in a bad news environment, and I went ahead and purchased the puts. You will be able to see in the next few days how good I am at playing my hunches on this. I have been right as many times as I have been wrong on playing these, but again, my backup is to get out at a small loss if the options go down or get out at a nice profit at some point in time.

One way or another you will be able see a hunch played out. I will see you on the other side of the trade.

Day 2: Friday, March 9, 2001
Krispy Kreme, W.I.N. Update

I started checking on Krispy Kreme (KKD) just to see how it was doing and I probably should have waited until today to buy the puts on this last little rise. This is what my stockbroker said to do. But because I get so busy sometimes and can't do all these trades, I went ahead and bought the puts yesterday. Once again, I will reiterate, if the stock does go to $80 or $82 before the split next week, I am definitely going to be buying some puts then. At that point in time I will be playing the April puts. (I am still in these).

Day 3: Monday, March 12, 2001
Krispy Kreme, W.I.N. Update

I was checking on Krispy Kreme (KKD). It is one of the few green lit up stocks on my stockbrokers' screen with so much of the market being down. Krispy Kreme is up around $80. If you go back to last week and remember the trade I did then, when the stock was around $77-$78. I went ahead and bought the $75 puts for March. Obviously, right now, I wished I had not have done that. In this case, my stockbroker was right. The stock did go up a little bit.

KRISPY KREME

March 8 - 13   Courtesy of Bloomberg, 2001

What I was thinking at that time, was the stock would rally into the stock split a few days in advance, and sure enough it has. I was also thinking it would back off right at the earnings announcement and give me a small profit in the put transaction. Instead, it went up and it did back off a little, but when it backed off, it only backed off to the price where it was when I purchased the put.

The stock has performed nicely rallying into the March 19th split and I still think it could go to $82 or $83. I am not going to sell out of my puts for this reason; even if the stock is at $82 on Friday, and it does the split, that will be two shares at $41. What I did was purchase more of the April puts. I purchased 10 contracts of the April $80 puts for $6.125 and 10 contracts of the April $75 puts for $3.875. I am going to load up, but again, this stock still may rally a little more into the split. I was very tempted to purchase the $80 calls for March, they were $1.9375, but I decided not to play those.

I am going to play the downdraft now with Krispy Kreme, and again, barring the fact that it might get taken over by Dunkin Donuts or some other such news, I think the stock will back off. I have a feeling that it might go down after the split. I am giving myself a month into the split for this to transpire and I am not playing the March options today.

DAY 4: TUESDAY, MARCH 13, 2001
KRISPY KREME FIRST W.I.N. UPDATE 8:14AM PST

Good morning everyone! This is Wade.

I just wanted to make another update on Krispy Kreme (KKD). I have an interesting and very strong comment to make, which is simply this; I would rather miss a trade than lose on a trade. I will come back to that in just a moment.

Remember what I was playing was not the rally into the split, I was playing a spike up in the price of Krispy Kreme after it's earnings announcement on March 7th. I remember mentioning on March 8th how risky playing the March puts would be because the expiration date was so short. Luckily I was able to get out today at a profit. The stock was at $77-$78 when I bought the March puts on March 8th, unlike yesterday's trades (April $80 put and April $75 put), which I placed when the stock was around the $80 range. I thought I could get out last Friday, but Krispy Kreme was one of the few bright shining spots, possibly due to its stock split this Friday. Again, it is doing a two-for-one split. If the other indicators look good, I still may play the rally into the split. At this time, I want to report that I got out of all four positions on the puts I had.

KRISPY KREME

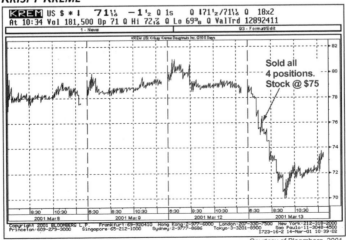

March 8 - 13

Courtesy of Bloomberg, 2001

1. I had purchased the March $75 puts, (they expire this Friday), for $1.50, and I think I got out at $1.6875 and picked up $0.1875. $300 doesn't sound like much, but it is better than losing money.

2. I also got out of the April $70 puts which I had purchased for $3.125 for $3.625.

3. The $75 puts for April on Krispy Kreme, which I had bought at $3.87; I got out of those at $5.625.

4. When the stock went up a little bit more, I bought ten contracts of the April $80 puts for $6, and I got out of those at $8.625.

When you add all that up, it is about $4,600 or $4,900 profit before commissions.

I am looking at Krispy Kreme rallying into the split, seeing if it will find a base here in the $75 range. Check this out; the $75 puts for March, which again will expire this Friday, were around $1.50. You are paying quite a bit for in-the-money on it, and I think the stock was at $75.25. The $70 calls were $5.375 x $5.50, which means they were virtually all intrinsic value, all in-the-money, and you are hardly paying any for time. Of course there is hardly any time left, only three or four days, but still if the stock goes up $1, that option is going to go up $1. It is almost going to be tick for tick, because you are buying a little bit deeper in-the-money call.

KRISPY KREME

March 8 - 13

Courtesy of Bloomberg, 2001

Yes, it costs more money and yes, you have more money at risk, but you also get a nice movement in the option compared with the stock price move.

DAY 4: TUESDAY MARCH 13, 2001
KRISPY KREME SECOND W.I.N. UPDATE 10:46AM PST

Hello everyone.

I was getting a bad signal from the road so I waited to get into the office and phone this up to the W.I.N. Department to record these transactions that I just did. I am going to give a further update on Krispy Kreme (KKD). I guess what you are going to hear now is about the fish that got away.

Last week I went fishing on Krispy Kreme. I was trying to play the earnings announcement thinking it was going to be a one- or two-day pop in the stock, which we did get up to the $78-$80 range. This was not the rally into the stock split.

I want to differentiate between the two:

1. The rally into the stock split should be today, tomorrow, Thursday and possibly into Friday. Buy puts if the stock gets up to $78 or $80. I am not sure that it will get up there again before the split because I think it is going to hit a pretty good support level around the $70-$75 range.

    Here is what happened with what I recorded this morning. I got out of the Krispy Kreme puts that I had purchased, and I got out too early. When I got into the car to drive to the office, the stock was down a little over $70. Now remember, I owned the $75 put, and when I got out of them, the stock was right around $75. It had dropped almost another $5. I could have sold those puts for about $4 or $4.50 more, and even on just the March puts, that would have been another $4,000 on the 10 contracts.

    So again, it is the one that got away, but as long as I have money in my pocket for lunch and a movie, I am a happy guy.

Count your blessings, just be happy and move on to the next deal.

2. The next deal could be a Krispy Kreme rally. What I did with the stock a little above $70 is buy the calls now on a one- or two-day trade rallying into the stock split coming up this Friday. Remember, the news on the earnings has played out, but we are possibly, after the big downturn in the market yesterday (Monday 3/12/01), heading into a little bit better marketplace as we get to March 15th. As people start to make better company reports, stocks should bottom out and start back up. That is a hopeful wish on my part. I don't see it happening too much.

However, with Krispy Kreme down around $70, I went ahead and purchased the $70 calls and the $75 calls. I think I paid $0.5625 for the $75 calls and by the time I had finished the trade, the stock had already moved up about $1. We had already covered the spread and made a little bit on that one, plus, I bought the $70 calls. I think they were $2.375, and I purchased ten contracts. I also purchased 40 contracts of the $75 calls.

Again, I am waiting for Krispy Kreme to get back up to $74, $75, $76, and I will be out of those probably tomorrow, maybe Thursday. This is the rally into the split and if the stock does get back up to the $76-$77 range, I am going to buy puts on it again for April or May into the split and wait for the downdraft after the split. What you are seeing here are trades about every couple of days. They seem to take that long to play out.

DAY 4: TUESDAY MARCH 13, 2001
KRISPY KREME THIRD AND FINAL (I PROMISE)
W.I.N. UPDATE 12:57PM PST

Hello everyone, it's me again.

It is just a few minutes before the market close, but I want to get one last final update on Krispy Kreme. I don't know

KRISPY KREME

March 8 - 13

Courtesy of Bloomberg, 2001

why I am so infatuated with this, because I still think it might rally a little bit more to the $74-$75 range.

I went ahead and cleared out of the call option positions that I bought this morning. I purchased the $70 calls for I think $2.375, and I just sold them for $3.50. On the $75 calls that I purchased when the stock was down in the mid $70 range, and now, with the stock up around the $72+ range, those $75 calls were going for around $1. I was able to get twenty contracts off at $1.0625 and another twenty contracts off at $1.1875. That is not a bad several hour trade. About $2,100 in and $4,200 out for a $2,100 profit in just a few short hours.

This was not the original intent I had when I went into the trade. I was going to hold it for a day or two, but I decided to go ahead and get out. You never know what the night-time will bring. All of a sudden maybe people will stop liking Krispy Kreme doughnuts.

By the way, I heard a great comment by a famous radio personality who said "Content, content, content." If you look at Krispy Kreme, it is a great company with incredible content. They have really good tasting doughnuts, so great content and great products bode well for the future.

Right now I am out of the trades, and on another pullback, I will get involved again, but that was a nice one-day trade. Again, this is a Stock Split Strategy #4A, Rally into the Split. I'm going to a movie!

Thursday, March 15, 2001
Krispy Kreme W.I.N. Update 8:29am PST

Good morning everyone! This is Wade.

I wanted to make some remarks in regards to Krispy Kreme (KKD). Krispy Kreme is not doing very well right now, and yesterday (Wednesday) I got so busy I couldn't record a lot of my transactions. I will tell you one we did try to do with Krispy Kreme.

I tried to buy twenty contracts of the April $70 calls, and all I got off was two of them. That is not a misprint, it was just two. I had eighteen that I did NOT get filled on because I had a limit order in and therefore I didn't spend that much money. At this point I am glad because the stock has backed off. I could have made just a little bit of money on them yesterday, because after I bought them, they did go up. I was waiting now for the one- or two-day rally into the stock split which will occur Monday (March 19th) and carry over until Tuesday.

If the stock drops down to the low $70 or the $69 range, I will probably jump in and try to do a quick one or two-day trade.

End of the Krispy Kreme trades at that time

KRISPY KREME   NOW KKD

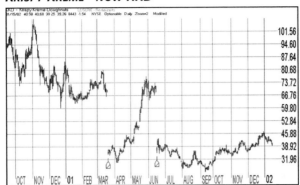

KRISPY KREME   (NOW KKD) MARCH 7-14, 2001

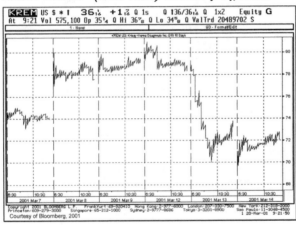

Courtesy of Bloomberg, 2001

KRISPY KREME   (NOW KKD) MARCH 7-20, 2001

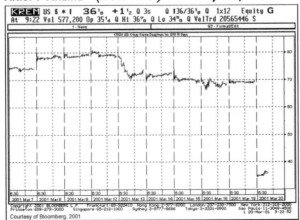

Courtesy of Bloomberg, 2001

DO NOT, I REPEAT, DO NOT DO TRADES ON A WHIM.
WISHFUL THINKING IS NOT A TRADING STYLE.

I would rather miss a trade than lose on a trade.
— WADE B. COOK

Note: You should make a separate copy of this page and carry it with you. This is to remind you of possible trades.

8

RED LIGHT, GREEN LIGHT
AND
STOCK SPLITS

Ilove stock splits, but there are special concerns and warnings on a few of the quick in and out plays. This chapter delves into enhancing each trade in regards to the five times to get involved and un-involved.

- Pre-Announcement
- On the Announcement
- Between the Announcement and the Split
- Rally into the Split and dip just AFTER (or During) the Split
- After Major Downturn – Play as Range Rider

Refer to page 166 of this chapter for more detail on the five times to watch for stock splits. It is also very important you read the transaction updates. You need to see real trades – hopefully we can make these trades come alive and be meaningful to you.

STOCK SPLITS

Stock splits present many interesting plays. I've outlined my five times to get in and out of stocks or options in the other volumes of this *Wall Street Money Machine Series* (Volumes 1-5).

I'll put a few reminders here, excerpted from these other books.

In *Wall Street Money Machine, Volume 4: Safety 1st Investing*, I have covered the times and strategies and highlighted some key points to watch for in companies that may be doing a stock split.

There are companies announcing stock splits all the time. They split their stocks to make their shares more affordable or to increase their float of stock.

I've seen so many stocks go from $90 down to $45 on a two-for-one split and go back up to around $90 within six to twelve months.

Once again though, what if you want to play these splits but you have limited resources? You can play options on the stock. Buying options on stock split companies minimizes the risks and lets you make a huge return in a short period of time.

I hope you've read between the lines and figured out that if there are five times to get in, there must be five times to get out. Don't ever go in the entrance until you know your exit. Again, to a different tune, once you know your exit, only then, should you go in.

Do your homework. Chart your own stock. Practice, observe, and practice some more.

Also, please note, one of my fellow instructors, Darlene Nelson and her husband, Miles, have specialized further and have put their strategies into a book called *Stock Split Secrets*.™ Pick this book up at a bookstore near you.

This book covers so much valuable information and strategies in regards to stock splits. Although I cannot cover them all in this chapter, I have highlighted a few of the strong points:

Stock Split Secrets shows the power of stock splits. Many stockbrokers may tell you that a stock split has no real impact on the value of a company. You might hear someone say, "When a stock splits, the share values are adjusted with no actual change in shareholder equity. A stock split is no reason to buy that stock."

When a company splits their stock they simply issue more shares of stock and distribute them to current shareholders. In a two-for-one stock split, a stockholder with one hundred shares of stock would receive an additional one hundred shares. Before the split, if one hundred shares of ABC stock are worth $10 each, the value of this holding would be $1,000. After a two-for-one stock split, ABC issues one hundred more shares of stock to the shareholder and the value of all shares is reduced to $5. Multiply two hundred shares times $5 it's still $1,000 – the result is no change in shareholder equity.

After well-known stocks split, they tend to increase in value until they have returned to the pre-split stock price. If you purchase shares in a strong company that has just split, you have the law of averages on your side. Chances are, if you purchase today and it splits two-for-one tomorrow, that stock will probably increase in value. Eventually it could be selling at a price equal to the pre-split price.

WHY DO COMPANIES DO STOCK SPLITS?

Understanding why companies do stock splits helps give us the power to profit from them.

When a company goes public, it is authorized to issue shares for sale on the open market. The shares of some companies are sold over the counter, on the NASDAQ, on the NYSE, and so forth. Over time, successful companies have a growing demand for their stock. The greater the demand, the higher the price per share. At times the demand far exceeds the supply and there is a shortage of available shares. This can cause very large and volatile swings in the price of the stocks. Eventually the company reaches a success point where they decide to do a stock split.

What follows are a few of the most common reasons that companies declare stock splits.

A. Increase Liquidity

B. Broaden Base of Stockholders

C. Increase Affordability

D. Pay Dividends Without Cash

Each time a stock split is completed the total number of shares increases – within a few years one hundred shares can multiply into

400 or even more. Over time, hopefully those shares increase in value, another stock split is announced, and the excitement continues.

In regards to Red Light, Green Light quarterly news periods, there are some very special considerations. First of all, the time period before the stock split announcement is often given at the same time as a lot of other news announcements, for example: earnings, dividends, share buy backs, and a host of other news-type events.

The beginning of the pre-announcement, the end of the quarter, and on to the actual SEC filings is a busy time. If the whole market is moving up, that up movement will only help. Your particular stock may benefit, even though its own good news is limited.

Also, remember that as stocks rise, the implied volatility of the option price diminishes. If you're playing options, a $4 stock move may translate into a $2 option move, but an additional $4 stock move may only move the option up $1. The next $4 move (nothing happens in even $4 increments – I'm using this hypothetical situation to make a point) of the stock may only see the option go up 50¢.

Note: the time value of the option deteriorates very rapidly as the expiration date nears. You could see the stock go up $4 over a week and the option hardly budge at all.

I share this information to help you make wiser decisions in choosing the strike price and the expiration month. You need time for the play to work! Yes, you'll get your biggest moves in the near-term options, but the added risk of a shorter expiration should make you stop and really consider the trade.

For example: A $46 stock moves to $50 in a few days. You own the $50 calls purchased for $3.50, and you own the $50 LEAPS® out in one and a half years, purchased for $11. With this $4 move, the $50 calls for next month go up to $6. The $50 LEAPS go up 50¢, to $11.50.

For cash now, the $50 calls for next month work nicely. But remember, the expiration date is imminent. If the stock doesn't move above $50, the $50 call strike price $6 option will deteriorate fast.

This is what I mean by, "Know your exit." You should know where you want out: either in a dollar move in the stock, a dollar move in the option (say $2) or a certain date. Time is your enemy when you purchase options.

Recently I had options on Microsoft. The stock started in the low $50s and climbed up $1 or so every few days, but my $60 options, which I had purchased a few weeks ago, were going nowhere. I barely got out at break even. The rise in price of the stock was working *for* me, but the time was working *against* me. Remember, there has to be enough time for the option to work.

Also remember, you need something to drive up the stock on calls, or drive down the stock on puts – the compelling reason if you will – or you should sit on the sidelines.

With the downtrending market that we have been experiencing the two years before I wrote this, a good trading arena has been to play puts on stocks as they actually do their stock splits – especially if the stock actually splits in the Red Light period. And it seems like the whole marketplace has been in a negative period as of late.

I've checked hundreds of charts on companies having done a stock split. It's amazing. I literally have not seen one stock price maintain the price as of the time of the split. In fact, I've seen many return to about the price where they were when the company announced the split.

Let me explain a typical scenario. A stock is at $60. The company is doing well. The stock climbs to $70 on hopeful pre-announcement news. At $70 the stock split announcement is made. The stock spikes up to $77, then backs off to $65. The split is in about forty days, a Friday.

The price goes up to $72, back to $69, then up to $73, back to $66, then back up to $72. That's one day's worth of activity. Just kidding, sort of. It could be over the forty days, but some of these stocks move like crazy. Look at the charts later in this chapter, and you'll see volatility in abundance.

Now, as the split date nears, you notice that it's the end of April. The news is out and 10-4 good buddy, it's over. The stock is at $74 just before the split, say three days. It rallies to $76 on Thursday. The split date is Friday, the ex-dividend date is on Monday. It's a two-for-one split. The stock opens at $38 and immediately spikes up to $39.50. By Thursday, with no news, it slips to $35, Friday it's back to $32, and $29 on Tuesday of the next week. If you had purchased this stock at $70, you would now wish you would have sold it at $76, pre split, or $38 times two, post split. After a few months this $29 stock could climb back to $35 or even more. What is needed? Another Green Light period, with good news.

Replay this situation with options. You purchased the May $70 calls for $4. It seemed like such a good idea. You bought ten contracts, and spent $4,000. After the split. You own twenty contracts of the May $35 calls. Wow, what seemed promising can backfire quickly. Sell the $35 calls on the way into the split, or if you're feeling frisky and risky, carry them to Monday, wait for the spike up and sell them for $5. Remember, the stock is at $39+. Get out, and get out of the way. Twenty contracts at $5 is $10,000, a nice $6,000 profit.

Tell me how you'll feel a few days later when the stock is at $32 and it's the Wednesday before the Friday expiration? The $35 calls are now $3. On Thursday, they're $1.50. On Friday there is "no bid." Zero, zip, nada.

BUY PUTS

One way to play this downdraft is to not only clear out of your stock call options, and even some spreads, but to buy puts.

A put gives you the right to sell stock at a set price. We don't necessarily exercise on the stock, we just sell our puts as they increase in value.

With the stock coming up on the split hits $74, right before the split, consider buying the $75 puts for $4. The $70 puts are just $2. The stock would have to go down significantly to make money. Let's use the same downdraft: After the split, the stock went up to $39.50 or $79, pre-split. Within days, it tanks to $35, $32, then $29. If we sold the $35 put when the stock was at $34, we'd make the intrinsic value, plus any time value left in the premium. There's not much there as the expiration is next Friday, only five days away. $2 is all we get, but that's $4,000. ($2 times twenty contracts equals $4,000.) $4,000 on $2,000 at risk is not a bad one-week trade.

Look at the charts starting on page 168. Notice that the stocks usually rise into the split, but notice the downturn right after the split. Hundreds of examples of this downturn, or dip, could be given for every one stock that splits and never goes below its pre-split price. This is a very important observation if you're playing options with a near-term expiration date.

A side note: one of the things I teach is that to make consistent money we have to quit making stupid mistakes. Holding positions through stock splits is usually a "not so smart" decision. Especially, I repeat *especially* if the stock split is in the actual Red Light period.

Yes, a Green Light news period can give added impetus to a stock moving up; I love rallies into the split in a news period, but a Red Light period can drown the sturdiest of facts. Play the compelling reason for the stock to go down. Buy a put, know your exit, make a small profit and go to the movies.

The following is a W.I.N. update on a company I recently followed into a stock split:

Day 1: American General Corporation (AGC)
Friday, March 9, 2001, W.I.N. Update 8:59am PST

Good morning everyone! This is Wade.

I just finished playing basketball and I wanted to call in to finish off the trade on American General Corporation (AGC). Even though it is down, I am going to repeat what I am doing with this play.

I am playing the two-for-one stock split which happened last week (Friday, March 2, 2001) over to Monday of this week (March 5, 2001). I am waiting for a bit of a downturn. I really think everyone should start practice trading some of these stock split downdrafts, into the split and right after the split. Checking virtually every chart of every stock that has done a split for the last year. You will see that it is an appropriate study area because in today's semi-negative marketplace, it seems to be easier to play the negative news than the positive news.

A company can have all kinds of good news, but if the marketplace is not going to let it take off, not letting it rise, we have to play the marketplace at hand, which is highly volatile in a particular trend area.

The play that I am doing on (AGC) is a two-for-one stock split. Here is what I purchased:

AMERICAN GENERAL CORPORATION

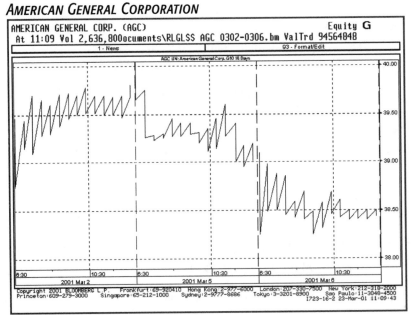

- When the time was right at the split date, I had purchased the $70 puts and the $75 puts. I paid $1.25 for twenty contracts of the $70 puts and $2.90 for twenty contracts of the $75 puts. A few minutes ago, the stock was at $38.49 and I need it to go down a couple more dollars before I will get out of that trade. I am almost to the breakeven point, but not quite there.

Day 2: American General Corporation (AGC)
Monday, March 12th, W.I.N. Update 8:59am PST

Good morning everyone! This is Wade.

I want to comment on my trades of this put buying strategy right at the stock split or right after the stock split. When American General (AGC) was in the $76-$78 range, I saw it rally into the split and I knew it was going to split down to two shares last Friday at around $39. I had previously purchased the $75 puts and the $70 puts which became the $37.50 and the $35 puts after the two-for-one stock split. The thought was that the stock, even though it might rally on Monday or Tuesday, would find some weakness. The thought was that the stock would go to $39 and then maybe dip down to $36 or $35 and I could get out with a double and possibly a triple on the put play.

I have been relatively successful at this as of late, and this was another put play on a widely traded stock. In other words, a large stock, hoping that it would go down right after the stock split like so many others have.

I am making these comments again right now to reiterate the statement that I make constantly in my Red Light, Green Light Home Study Course. It is simply this:

1.   The stocks move in anticipation of a news event.

2.   Stocks move at the news event based on the quality of the news.

3.   Stocks move also in tandem with the marketplace in general.

At this point, you would think this stock would be moving down, but remember point #2: The quality of the news. Here we are a week or so later, and Prudential (PLC), a European company, makes an announcement that it is going to buy American General. Looking at this, I see the stock up at $40+, which is $80 price pre-split, and obviously for purchasing puts, it is not going the right way. I guess that is just the luck of the Irish. I don't know if I am going to get out of this trade at a profit with all of this good news coming out.

Ironically, as you look at point #3: The movement of the whole market, we are seeing an incredibly down market both on the NASDAQ and on the Dow. You would think that this stock would be swept down with the marketplace in general. With AGC, my stockbroker said it is one of the few green spots on his screen with a lot of blood, or a lot of blood with a lot of the other stocks going down. Again, bad luck this time.

I only have a few thousand dollars tied up in the trade and the stock price could, with the purchase of the company out there, go down and I still own the April puts. We will see what becomes of those. Maybe I will net a profit or get close to breaking even on both the March and the April trades.

The following is excerpted from *Wall Street Money Machine, Volume 4: Safety 1st Investing.*

FIVE TIMES TO WATCH FOR COMPANIES THAT MAY BE ANNOUNCING STOCK SPLITS

1. **Pre-announcement.**

- They run in groups.
- Buy at-the-money calls, buy slightly out-of-the-money calls.
- They historically split at certain times or prices.
- Sell Puts at certain times or prices.
- They have a shareholder meeting to authorize more stock (usually for a split).
- Watch for roll ranges.
- Probably do options with expiration dates after the split date.
- Other news.

2. **On the announcement.** Be careful.

- Stocks spike up.
- Watch out. Options rise dramatically. If you chase it, you'll get burned.
- If you don't catch it within seconds, wait for #3.

- This is my least favorite.
- Don't place market orders – only place limit orders.
- The stock and options are too volatile.
- If option spikes up, consider sitting it out. Wait for a better play.

3. **Between announcement and the split date.**

- Wait a few hours or days after the announcement.
- Give options a chance to settle down.
- This time is usually four to six weeks.
- Watch for roll patterns.
- If the stock has had a quick run up it may back off. Look for other news.
- Many stocks roll up and down based on other news.

4. **Into the split.**

- Many stocks pull back the week of the split, but by Friday (split date), it runs up.
- Buy call options, sell put options into the split. Say, Wednesday then sell Friday (Ex-dividend date is Monday).
- Many stocks fall several dollars after split – Monday following Friday split.
- Sell everything.
- Buy again in #5.

5. **After the split.**

- Wait a few days.
- Consider buying put on split date.
- Many stocks lull around for a few weeks, or months. Wait for news sometime as we head into the next quarter.
- Look for roll patterns.
- Consider LEAPS if you like the stock. Buy on dips.

Most of my students know I am a student of stock splits. Our research is not only never ending, but quite intense. Let me share with you several of our observations of the past few years. As you read and ponder these movements, I hope you too will explore the cause and effects as well as how to play the effects – hopefully causing you to make more money.

KRISPE KREME

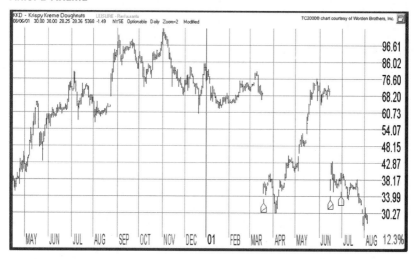

CITRIX SYSTEMS

INTEL CORP

NORTEL NETWORK HOLDINGS

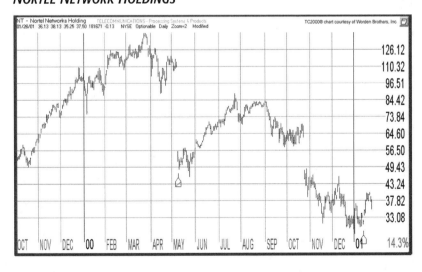

SUN MICROSYSTEMS, INC

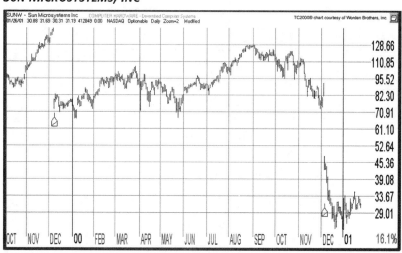

CISCO SYSTEMS, INC.

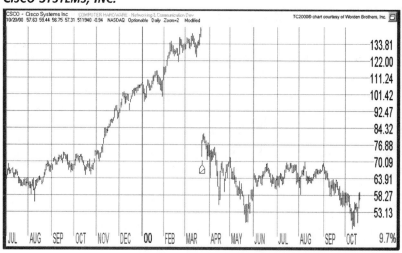

DOWNDRAFT AT THE SPLIT

A few years ago, I was showing several charts to a class in Florida. I don't even remember what the topic was. Serendipity strikes whenever she wants. I noticed that every stock split chart had an interesting dip downward at the split or shortly thereafter. It was disturbing at first, as are all things when they don't fit the pattern.

Here's what would happen. A stock is at $105. A two-for-one split announcement is made and it spikes up $4 to $109 (more on this in point #3). It backs off, shoots to $115, then down to $109 then up to $118. The week of the split it's back to $109. It's been almost six weeks. It's Wednesday. The stock rallies the week of the split to $112 and on Monday the shares open at $56. By 10:00AM, the stock is at $54. Wednesday it goes down to $52.40 That's even lower than where it was when they announced the split.

Look again at the charts on page 185-187 and you'll see the dips; here are just six. I could show you a thousand others. Only once in a while do they keep going up. I mean, very, very seldom. So I figure it this way. If I've sold out at a profit, there will be times to buy back in, but maybe not at a really low price. I've only found a few which did not dip on the split. On the others I've sold out of every call option, bought back every sold put (naked) option, wound out of every spread and sold every stock.

Here is a transcription of part of a CD I taped before a trip to London the week before a Microsoft split. I was right on on this one. Oh, how I wish I would have sold my Dells.

EXCERPT FROM WIN

Now I discovered something about six months ago. Actually I discovered it about a year and a half ago and I've just let it mull around in my brain. Something started to gel in my mind as I watched companies come up on stock split times and things like announcements of share buybacks. This is where the Red Light, Green Light phenomenon comes into play.

I've noticed that around, say January, that there are a lot of companies talking about what they are doing. Remember, December

31st is the calendar quarter and also the year end. Towards the end of January, when they actually start doing their SEC filings – remember they have ninety days – a lot of these companies come out with earnings reports.

They also come out with different things the company is going to do. Remember the board of directors just met, it's the end of the year, and they get to discuss the money that they've made, what they're going to do with the money. They also start disseminating a whole bunch of newsy type things. So the end of January, as you get kind of one month into a filing period or at the end of the filing period, you'll notice a whole bunch of newsy things coming out from the company. I'm going to talk about a negative aspect of this in just a second, but you'll see share buyback numbers, you'll see all kinds of stock split announcements.

Look what happened at the end of January 1999. The first part of February we had Microsoft announce a two-for-one split. Sun Microsystems was the first one with a two-for-one split, then IBM announced a two-for-one split, and Intel. Whether they were going to do the split right away or within a few weeks or several months out, they all came out with the announcements at relatively the same time. That's the key, the anticipation of this kind of news. It's out there; there are whisper numbers and whisper information about what's going on with the company. So the end of January brings just a huge amount of news by all kinds of companies, from Xerox to McDonalds to AOL. Now the stock splits weren't actually going to happen until March, the end of March or even in April, right? That's when the stock splits were actually going to happen. Some of those that announced in January aren't even going to split until May, but the stocks started going crazy.

Almost all the stocks that I just told you about went up $5, $10, $15, $20. And boy, did Microsoft go up, around $170. Dell Computer got up around $110, IBM was way up there in the $190-$200 range, and Intel was around $130 or $136. After the stocks went up, something happened. The stock split announcement was already made. The stock splits once again were out three weeks, six weeks, eight weeks, ten weeks away, and virtually every stock I just mentioned backed off. Why? The market is doing OK, moving up towards 10,000 on the Dow, so why? Why did they back off? I'm going to say it very succinctly, and then I'm going to try to explain it the best that I can. Because there was no more news. The news had played out. So what do we need? To have those stocks go back up and our LEAPS® go back up and our options go back up, <u>we</u> <u>need</u> <u>more</u> <u>news</u>.

Now remember, the stock market is either going up, down or sideways. They can be going sideways with an upward bent to it, so we could have a range rider effect with the whole stock market or any particular stock. Let's get back to this. We need more news. I want you to start thinking about this news, not from your perspective from the outside looking in, but look at the process from the inside out. Go into the minds and look through the eyes of the insiders of the company; the CEO and the CFO. What can they say? What can they not say?

All right now, let's take time out here. Even if they've announced stock splits and the stocks go down during that time, what happens? What happens if they actually do their stock split, like on March 5th and 6th and 7th like Dell did? What happens? The stock splits. There are several plays here I want to discuss with you, but often the stock splits in a no-news period. For example, the month of May might be a slow news period, but here's the question: "I want to buy this option, but should I buy this option right now?" I say, "Excuse me, what is the compelling reason why this stock and therefore the option should go up?" What is the compelling reason? Because if you're expecting news and good earnings to come out, don't expect these through the month of February, the month of May, the month of September or from about the middle of August until September and about let's say the end of October until mid-December. If you could look at these things on charts and look at these companies you'll see an incredible phenomena. Are you seeing the picture? I'm going to explain it again because I want to make sure that you understand this.

Let's relate some of these to where some of you are. You look at Dell and think, well after the stock did a split on March 5th or 6th it spiked up there a little bit, and it's going to take a dip down to say $42 from say $45. What I'm saying is that at that point in time on March 5th, until the middle of March there is no news. Now ironically during this time, a couple of weeks ago I was doing a speaker training with seventy of our speakers who are teaching our seminars. I was sharing information on Microsoft with them on a Monday, March 15th and Tuesday the 16th. I said we're coming up to the middle of March and we're entering the news period. Microsoft is not doing the split until the end of this month but watch us enter this news period, and wham! All of a sudden, within that same day, Microsoft was thinking about settling the lawsuit with the government. A couple of hours later, Microsoft announced it was dividing the company into four groups and a lot of people are thinking that's in anticipation of a split up. I don't think that that will happen. Then the next day on the 16th, Microsoft was expected to beat its estimates. You see the point? The news starts fresh, the news starts all over. With all the news about Microsoft (there wasn't any almost all the way through the month of February), what did the stock do? The stock went from $170 down to $145, hung around there $148, $153, back to $140. It hung around there for a long time until you come up on the anticipation of the new news period.

Remember, there are a lot of players who know a lot of things about Microsoft; the analysts that follow it every day and have access to information that we don't even have access to. They start the anticipation. Remember, buy on rumors sell on news. The anticipation of the news being good drives the stock price up. Dell had the exact opposite effect; even going into the split there were a lot of people saying that they weren't going to hit their earnings numbers. Others thought that they were going to be right at estimates, and they were. They're still making a lot of money, it's still a great company, but the stock got slammed. It was up at $110 and it went clear down to $75, $76. Now it kind of rallied right before the news and got back up to $82, $84 and then it did a split, two-for-one. And now the stock was around $44, $45 and even at the time of this recording it had backed off to right around $36. Thirty-six dollars, guys, that's $72 pre-split. I rest my case.

I was sharing this with my wife, who's a pretty savvy investor too, and when I got done she just stared at me. She was looking at me and said, "You know Wade, what helped you discover this was the fact that you are the CEO of a publicly-traded company, and you're trying to teach people what goes on in the stock market. Your observation of this is based on your first hand knowledge of what you can and cannot do as a CEO of a publicly traded company." And I said, "You know, you're right." That's what made me start thinking about all of it. So a lot of you ask, "Why didn't I think of this?" Well, because that really wasn't your position. I mean you are not a president of a publicly-traded company so you would not naturally think of these things, but I have to think of these things all the time. Then I started to relate what goes on in the stock market: news, no news, news, no news. What is the compelling reason for a stock to go up? If all the news is played out, all the earnings reports, share buybacks, stock splits, all those kinds of newsy announcements have happened and the stock ran up sometimes even in anticipation of those types of news items, then it goes into a quiet period for thirty to forty-five days.

Even in the new Wall Street Workshop™ I'm going to revise a lot of what we're teaching to reflect that. After stock split strategy #4 going into stock split strategy #5 that yes, it may be two or three or four days after the stock actually does this split that it takes a little downturn but sometimes, a lot of times, it doesn't recover until the next news period. Which is in many cases about thirty to forty-five days away.

I'll try to be more specific here: a news period will end about three to four weeks at end of a calendar quarter. It will actually start about two weeks before the next quarter. So for example with the March 31st calendar quarter the news will start around March 15th. It will go until about April 15th when all the reports have actually come out. Some companies move towards April 20th, and then from about April 20th to April 25th on through the month of May up until the middle of June, there will be a quiet period.

Things die down. Not every company performs exactly like this, because some companies may have different calendar quarters. You need to find out what each company has as a year end and its calendar quarter. Then wait for the next newsy period which will start about the middle of June and go through about the end of July. Then a lot of stocks are going to have a hard time again, all the way from the end of July through August until the middle of September.

Around the middle of September, all the news picks up again. Most companies start to put their best foot forward. This goes through October. Then the last week of October and all through November is another quiet period with stocks having a hard time until mid-December going into the Christmas season and year end.

After the first few days of December, there is usually a serious dip, and then a rally into the year end (except 1997). I've taken the one month of December off of a 12 month chart and have placed this one month in side by side rows, you can learn a lot by looking at these charts.

EDITED UPDATE

So here's what I did with this observation. Armed with what I, as a CEO, know about the filing periods and what I can and cannot do and can and cannot say, I went to our Research and Training Department (a great team of research people) and I said, "Here is my theory. Here is my hypothesis. Here is what I have observed. Prove me right or prove me wrong. Is my observation right or wrong? If my observation is right, then tens of thousands of people are going to use this information on the timing of their option plays, maybe even the timing of their stock plays. Why buy a stock at $88 if, after the end of a news period, you could buy it at $82 when the news is played out?" People are going to get better at this process. This also could possibly make the SEC take a look at the whole filing period and what goes on there. I don't know how they're going to adjust it, but I think everybody in every major company needs to look at the effect they have on the news that they disseminate, good or bad.

For us though, as Wall Street Workshop™ graduates, how do we learn to play this? This could be really, really important. I told my Research and Training Department, "I want you to make a fair test of the Dow Jones 30. I want you to look back for one year. Look at charts on how stocks rally into these news periods. Do they rally into this news period, kind of hang around the news period, go up or down a little based on the quality of the news, good or bad, and then at the end of that period of time what happens to them? Then I want you to take the S&P 500, take company #1, #11, #21, #31 on down; that will give us fifty companies to look at. Within three or four days we had our preliminary reports back and my Trading Department told me, "Wade, this is amazing! This is just amazing! As you look at all of these things together, you can almost take transparencies of all these Telechart 2000® type charts, and if you adjust them for their different calendar quarters and lay them on top of each other you definitely see a pattern." I am proposing it to you. I am in the middle of the research on this myself. I am starting to use it in my trading period for example. I'm going to tell you another quick strategy and then I'm going to kick myself in the fanny and tell you what I did and what I didn't do. Then I'll get back to this news period, this quarterly filing newsy-go-round. "It's a quarterly filing newsy-go-round." By the way, I think that newsy-go-round sounds a lot like merry-go-round, and I don't think that's a dissimilar comparison. Look at a merry-go-round. Horses on a good merry-go-round go up and down as the merry-go-round goes around from one quarter to another.

Let's take a whole year of going around in a circle to get back to March 31st. Let's say the horses, these stocks, are going up and down. While they're down, we need to be buying. While they're up, we need to be selling. And see, as the merry-go-round goes around, as the calendar quarter goes around, the stocks go according to the news and the quality of the news about them. They definitely have news periods and then no-news periods and often we buy when we should be selling, and vice versa. Sometimes we're buying an option right in the middle, like a one-month-out option for example, right in the middle of April. It's heading into the no-news period from April through May, and we're wondering why the option didn't pan out. Why, when the company looked like it was going to go from $88 up to $100 and we bought the $90 call option, and the stock went down to $87, down to $86, down to $85? In desperation we ask, "Why isn't this stock turning around?" Well, why should it?

Here's the question again: what compelling reason does this stock have to go up? What is driving the price up? And as it starts to leak down a lot of people start to sell it to $88, to $87, to $86. It kind of takes on a momentum of its own. But if it's in this negative or no-news period, what is the compelling reason for it to go up? I'm asking all of us to take a hard look at this phenomena as we're doing our paper trades, our practice trades, even our real trades. Ask the question, why am I buying this? Why should this thing go up? What is driving it up? Am I buying it at the end of all the good news? You see, buy on rumors, sell on fact. A lot of us are buying on fact because we think that there's going to continue to be more good news. And I'm saying let's really be careful, because there are actual no-news periods, periods of time in each quarter when the company can't talk about itself, or when there is no new news. We should not try to fight against the downward trend when the company does not make any announcements, or when it is in a no-news period.

All right, now let's talk about Dell and stock split strategy #4. We're coming up on the Dell stock split and the expiration date in the month of March. Now most of you know one of my favorite strategies is stock split strategy #4 and I'll explain it very quickly. One or two days before the actual stock split, let's say that the split day, the pay date, is going to be Friday. The ex-dividend date, the actual date that two shares are going to show up in your account for each one that you owned will be on Monday. The stock has run up to $88 and right before the stock split it's backed off to say $82 or $83 on Tuesday or Wednesday. What I've noticed a lot of times is that the stock rallies into the split; it will go back up from $84 to $86 to $87. It may not get back up to $88, but I have seen it many, many times rally into the split. So let's say that it does, it rallies to let's say $86. Well, how do you play that? Tuesday or Wednesday before the split, if it's on a dip and you've done your homework, you say, "What's the compelling reason now?"

The compelling reason is a lot of people are loading up. They're trying to get involved in the stock split. So you look at the $80 calls or the $85 calls even one month out. Go out a little further for even more insurance. But you look at these calls and say, "My goodness, the $80 calls are $5 and the $85 calls are $3." You buy ten contracts. You spend $5,000 or $3,000. You buy ten contracts and sure enough, that stock goes from $83 and rallies up during that week to $86 and your $5 becomes $6. Your $3 becomes $4.50 and bam! Your $3,000 is now $4,500 and you're out. You made a nice little profit for the three days.

Now let's watch what happens on Monday. On Monday, the stock is split down to two shares at $43 and many times it even opens up at $43, $43.50, or $44. Once in a while, even for a day or two, if there's all kinds of other good news and if the stock market is doing really well, it may even go up to $44 or $45. But by Wednesday or Thursday many times it's back down to $39. Many, many times I've seen these stocks split at $86 down to two shares at $43 and they open up on Monday at $41. They close at $86 on Friday but they open up down, depending on a lot of other things in the market.

What I started doing, especially with all of my near term options, was to rally them into the split and sell on that Friday. The exact timing is a little hard. You can wait until the end of the day, but it's hard to guess. Sometimes when the stock has rallied to $86 and it's 10:00 in the morning and you sell right now, and it goes to $88 by the end of the day, you missed out a little bit on your profits. I'm telling you what I'm doing. We are getting out of these options and even the stock.

About three or four months ago, after observing this happening with hundreds and hundreds of companies, I said to my stockbroker, "On the split date, the trading day in advance of the ex-dividend date, I want out of everything. Unload everything." I told all my stockbrokers, "If I tell you I want to keep 1,000 shares of stock, slap me. I want to sell and get rid of it."

Well now let's talk about Dell. I sold my March options and I sold some April options and I made some really, really good money. But Dell was sitting there around $82, $83 the week before the split. It rallied up in to the $85, $86 range and split down to two shares at around $42 or $43. Dell even went up for the next two or three days, to around $45. Now that's equivalent to $90 pre-split. I should have sold right there. I mean, after the two-for-one splits, I have like 15,000+ shares of Dell. I had over one hundred LEAPS® on Dell, which now means I have two hundred. I had 100 of the $90s, now I have two hundred of the $45 LEAPS®, and I had short-term options. I had all kinds of positions on Dell and I could have sold everything and made hundreds of thousands of dollars. Now I did sell all of my short-term options and was very profitable on those, but I kept saying, "Well, I'm not really doing Dell for the short-term, I'm going Dell for the long-term." Well guess what? I came into the studio just a few minutes ago, I called my stockbroker before I got into the studio here, and Dell was right around $36.50. That's $72. I could have sold virtually 15,000 shares at $45. Well, I'm just going to hang onto Dell for the long-term, hang onto these LEAPS®, but I could have sold every bit of stock. I knew this strategy. I knew it was going to happen and I didn't do it. Are any of you like me?

I think that we all need to monitor our accounts better, read our accounts better, and learn and practice trade the formulas. Now, at the time of this tape recording, you'll be able to see if I'm a genius or whether I'm not a genius as I get ready to go to London. Coming up this Friday is the Microsoft stock split. I've been telling my stockbroker if it gets to $176 to $180, or anywhere in the $180s, up to $190 on Friday – which is the split date – and Monday is the ex-dividend date, March 26th, by March 29th, I want to be out of everything. I mean every position, every LEAP, every spread, everything on Microsoft as it rallies up into the split. I want to sell everything. If we were under water on a few of the short-term options, which we're not, but even if we were, get out.

The news that drives the stock up or down is news usually about the financial facts of the companies, but in advance of this news is the anticipation of the news. Often, the anticipation of a news event drives the stock more than the actual news.

We have a lot of things I would like to discuss with you, but we don't have that much time left so I'm going to have to quickly go through some things. I have some more ideas on the stock market to cover. I've got another trade I'm going to tell you about, but first I'm going to give you this quote:

> *Discovery consists of seeing what everybody has*
> *seen and thinking what nobody has thought."*
> —ALBERT SZENT-GYORGYI NAGTRAPOLT

I encourage all of you to never give advice to other people, even if your friends ask you to. They may ask, "What do you think the hot stock is today?" You say, "Microsoft." Don't say that. Tell them a strategy, tell people the truth, tell them what you have done and then teach them a strategy, but don't recommend stocks. Can you imagine that stock going south and then they come back and blame you? Quit giving advice. I don't give advice. You shouldn't give advice. We teach people correct ways of doing things and then they govern their own actions.

Let's get back to practicing trading for a second and then I'm going to talk to you about your friends. I suggest that on every strategy – stock split strategy #4, Rolling Stocks, Rolling Options, doing IPOs, whatever – that you do at least fifteen trades on each strategy before you actually use real money. I think out of those fifteen trades, ten in a row should be profitable, which means if you do nine trades in a row and then you have a loser, start all over again, on paper. Don't use real money until you have such a lock on a particular strategy that you've got it figured out.

The next thing about practice trading is to go back to practice trading anytime the marketplace or any particular stock substantially changes. If the Dow goes like last summer from 9200, 9400 clear down to 7500, then go back to paper until you have it all figured out again. If a stock runs from $100 up to $300, go back to paper because is it going to be able to sustain that price? Instead of thinking that it's $300 going to $400, practice trade it so you're learning all the time.

The last thing is this: a lot of you, I know, have limited resources and I appreciate that because I try to keep my view as a cab driver in everything that I teach. But if you have $4,000 or $5,000 to invest and you've practice-traded a certain strategy and then you actually invest your hard cold cash into that strategy and your money is gone, it's tied up for three weeks until the next expiration date, keep paper trading. Five a day; that's a good rule by the way, five trades a day, either real or paper. Why? Because it's like doing lay-ups, five trades a day so that after the expiration date and your money is freed up, you don't have to start your research process again to find good companies or good bull put spreads or whatever you have been practicing. You know what's working on paper, you're just waiting now for the money to get freed up and then you're ready to go buy. Doing five trades a day, real or paper, you'll stay in the game and you'll be sharper when it's time to trade.

You know a lot of you came to the Wall Street Workshop™, and you may think that that's the end, but the Wall Street Workshop™ is the beginning. It takes a lot of fuel to get a rocket ship off the ground. You've seen those go, right, with the huge tanks of fuel? Well once the rocket ship gets out into space it hardly needs any fuel at all, but a lot of you are still in that thrust stage of trying to get up and get off the ground and get going. We've created the Next Step.™ This event is selling out all around the country. I encourage all of you to take and retake the FYI™ (Fortify Your Income™). It's billed out at $1,695 but you get one free with the Wealth University™ package, so please, please, take the FYI™.

These dips are almost predictable. At least they happen on cue. Because of this, the entrance and exit points are visible – clearly defined. This fact alone makes it easy to play and win. Also note; puts build value faster than calls in many situations as stocks usually retreat faster than they advance.

This observation on quick playing stocks splits was actually not my first observation. Before I give you observation two, let me give you the prequel: Stock Splits – episode one.

More Thoughts On Stock Splits

I also guess because of the popularity of my books and seminars that many other people have sat up and taken notice. Today there is much more interest in splits – the anticipation, the news announcements, the type: two-for-one, three-for-one, five-for-four, three-for-two, ten-for-one, and the dates. I still submit it's an area of cash flow investing worthy of study, practice and trading.

Before I move on, I was on a plane to Orlando to speak at one of our Semper Financial™ Conventions. I asked our Research and Training department for about ten charts of companies which split recently – at least two to three weeks before I left. The charts had to be of one month length and go a few weeks after the split. I'm including all ten of them here. My staff did not know why I wanted them. These are amazing in that they prove my point so well. I'll use them for point number one and some of them later for point number two.

1. Is this amazing or what? The stock splits and falls.

Exxon Mobil Corporation

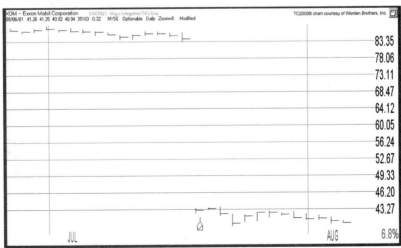

2. The stock went up slightly but then backed off in a week or so.
   I've never said all stocks fall. I've also never said all stocks fall on
   the dates of the split. To be cautious, I get out on the pay-date, I
   don't wait for the ex-dividend date.

LOWE'S COMPANIES

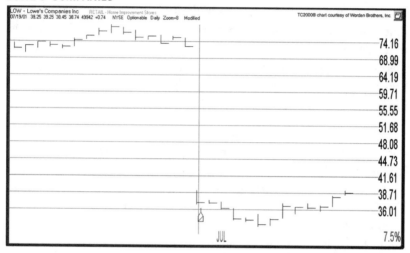

3. Another one that rallies into the date then falls at the open on
   Monday.

METRO ONE TELECOM, INC.

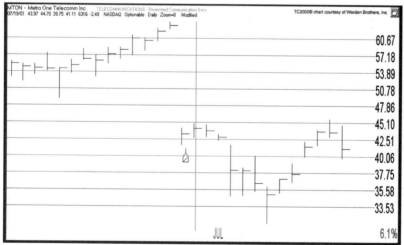

4. Are you seeing how to make money with this? Calls before, puts upon the split? Keep studying this phenomenon.

FIRST HEALTH GROUP CORP.

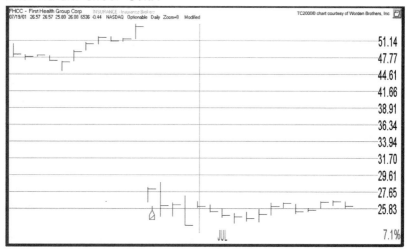

5. Another great example. Bull put spreads right before may be costly to unwind or close out. Consider Bull calls.

LINCARE HOLDINGS INC.

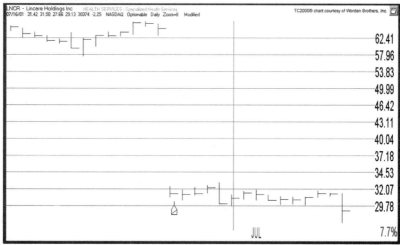

6. Up and Down: Patterns that look like a roller coaster are easy to play.

EXPRESS SCRIPTS INC.

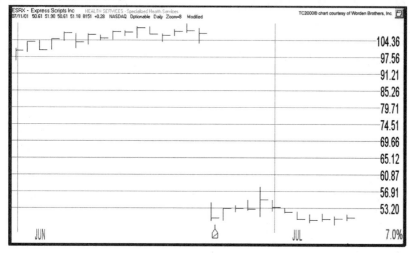

7. The examples keep coming. Look at this rally for a few weeks, then the down turn.

SHUFFLE MASTER INC.

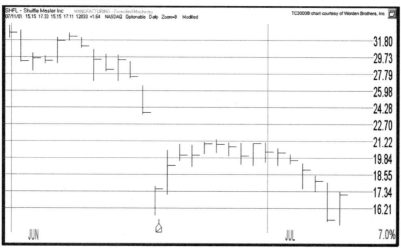

8. Rapid or slow – it happens. Check the no-news period.

CHEESECAKE FACTORY INC.

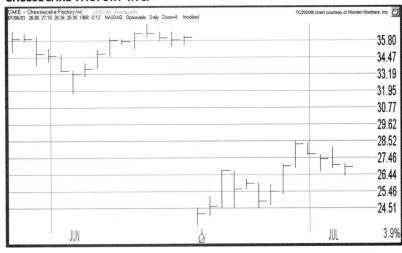

9. Look how this one came down the few weeks before the split (Red Light period?), then a brief rally and quick turnback.

FUELCELL ENERGY INC.

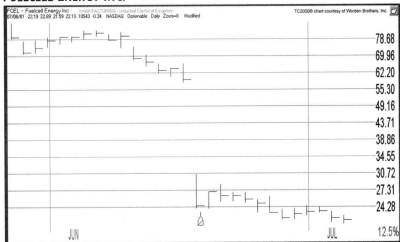

10. Observation, trends, patterns, practice. Become an expert.

DIAGNOSTIC PRODUCTS INC.

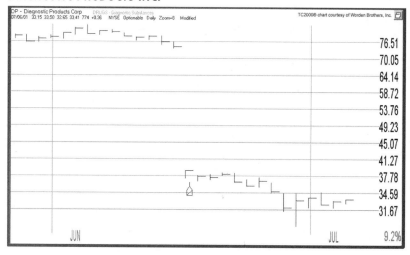

I could almost rest my case for point number one with these ten charts. But our observation work is never done. We'll, make reference to the same previous charts and use others as we explain a second unique way to capture profits.

KRISPY KREME

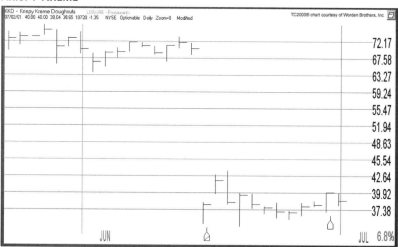

APPLEBEE'S

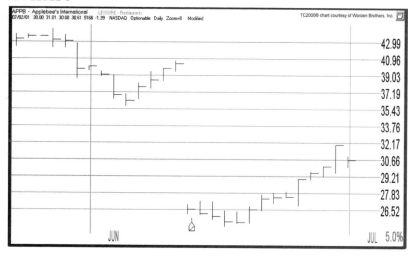

JOHNSON & JOHNSON

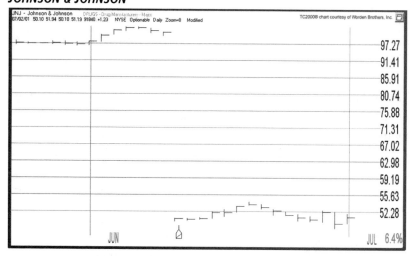

LABORATORY CP AM HOLDINGS

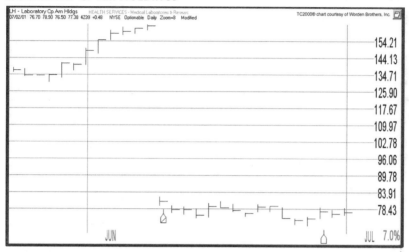

You would have to be an ostrich with your head buried in a Wall Street manhole not to see a lot of volatility between the time a company announces a stock split and when the stock actually splits. This time period could be four weeks to several months. In fact, if you've read my Red Light, Green Light investment course, this time could go through one or two periods of each.

To begin, no one has ever said to jump right in on the announcement. That time is just one of five times – and probably the time most fraught with danger. That will be dismissed in point number three. The announcement could be the start of a sharp rise. It could create a quick run-up in the stock. I've seen stocks fall several dollars on the announcement. Again, we'll cover that point later. The point here is that the split process goes into phase two. Oh how I wish I could have written phase one but it seems like way too many people know about the split way before the announcement. Part of the explanation is the fact that the stock split announcement is accompanied by many other newsy type things. In fact, the announcement is preceded often by much speculation of these other things.

Briefly let me list a few news items analysts and investors everywhere follow. These usually come out right around the time the

Board of Directors meets or right after, before, or sometimes at the shareholder meetings.

News that is worth following:

1. Earnings – good or bad

2. Share buybacks

3. Dividends

4. Mergers – takeovers, spin-offs

Just look at the previous four charts. The weeks before the stock split announcement should cause concern. Be careful.

A rapid rise to me spells a pullback. Look at the trendline and other volatility factors after the announcement.

CLEAR OUT

Almost every time I keep these options, stocks, or spreads through the split, I regret it. Sometimes I could have made more money on Monday or Tuesday, but overall closing out those positions would have made me more money. There are always other buying opportunities.

There are other plays but let's review. Here's what I do.

1. Buy calls on dips – sell into rally right before split.

2. Wind out of bull put spreads.

3. Keep bull call spreads in place if significantly out of the money. Otherwise close positions.

4. Sell stock.

5. Buy puts.

6. Implement bear call spreads – careful of the Internet or other high-flying stocks.

That's it. Simple, direct. Cash flow now. These are also easy to practice.

Where are you with all this? On the "Passion-Precision-Profits" line–where are you?

Look at the chart of IBM. I'll also list my trades on the next few pages. Have I always cleaned out of these trades? No! Many times though this strategy has worked. I'm sort of a classic case of "Physician heal thyself." Did I say I wished I would have sold Dell on the last split?

IBM

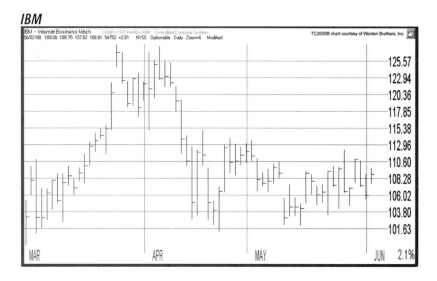

STOCK SPLIT ANNOUNCEMENTS–DANGER

Many people try to play stocks or options right on the announcement. As a long-term investment–say three or four years–this may be an okay trade. As a short-term cash flow formula there are special concerns–especially if you're playing call options.

Sometimes a press conference is called. Sometimes out of no-where the stock split announcement is made. The shareholder meeting is set to authorize more shares, the CEO or others start talking about a stock split. There is no big secret to splits. In theory the value of your stock is the same after the split as before. One hundred shares at $140 are now two hundred shares at $70. No big deal.

Announcements are often made after hours – at the end of the day or before the market opens. Sometimes these news events happen intra-day.

I have noticed an unusual and scary occurrence. The stock is at $142. It's May. The July $145 calls are currently $9. The announcement is made. The stock goes to $144. The options go to $13. How can this be? In theory it should be the opposite. If the stock goes up $4 the options should rise $2, not the other way around.

Option market makers set prices. They know a lot of people play stock splits. Volume increases. They can reset their volatility number in their computers, and change prices in a few seconds at the higher price.

If you choose this option, say with a market order, you will get filled at the higher price. Later in the day the stock backs off a dollar or so and the option price declines dramatically. It may never recover before the option expiration date.

Option prices are made up of three basic components.

1. Any intrinsic value or the portion of the option premium which is above the strike price of a call, or below the strike price of a put.

2. Time value – the length of time to option expiration.

3. Implied volatility – a fancy way of saying "what someone thinks" the movement, up or down, could be. If there's a really high likelihood the stock may rise or fall dramatically then the option price will be higher, for both calls and puts.

In short, option market makers are not stupid. If they can sell an option for $13 why should they sell it for $8? It's really that simple!

Your caution is to be careful. Maybe it would be better to get involved a few hours or days later. Seldom does the stock shoot straight up. Even at that, they back off. Like buses, another one will be by shortly.

Another play would be to sell the call. Let's say the stock runs up to $148. At that price the $150 call for June is $10. A nice premium. Careful, though, you'd be selling a naked call.

EXCERPT FROM RESEARCH AND TRAINING

Let's go on with more of our profits – this is from our Research and Training Department.

Our boss, Wade Cook, is a savvy Wall Street trader. Years of investing have given him the insight that as a company's quarterly reporting period approaches, news about the company increases, and this dynamic may cause upward pressure on the stock price. In Wade's pattern, a company initiates a two to four week price trend by generating published reports and holding news conferences leading to the posting of its quarterly earnings report. Wall Street experts, called analysts, present their neutral views. These specialists analyze the company's data and publish their own views on how the company is doing. Their comments include expectations which a company must meet to show that it is on target, and this is how a company justifies the price valuation of its stock. When the company misses the analysts' "number," the price of its stock often corrects to a lower level. As this high-profile, "newsy" activity increases and corresponding to whether the news is positive or negative, the price of the stock will trend up or down leading to the posting of the quarterly earnings report. Having made these observations, Wade asked the Research and Training Department at Wade Cook Financial to study this market phenomenon. The following paragraphs illustrate Wade's observations about company news and quarterly earnings, which the department was able to confirm and detail. Dell Computer Corporation (DELL) will serve to model the pattern.

DELL's quarterly period ended January 31, 1999. Earnings were posted on February 16th. As the quarterly period drew to a close, the volume of positive "newsy" items increased and the stock rose to a new high at $110 a share. Market sentiment anticipated a positive earnings report and a possible stock split announcement. DELL also rose on the rumor that it was about to launch an expansive Internet venture to increase online sales. After January 31st, DELL drew back in price as if to catch its breath and consolidate for a move up on the announcements. On February 10th, Wade Cook entered the public trading area at the Semper Financial™ Convention in Los Angeles, where the Research and Trading Department was projecting a Bloomberg real-time options chain for Dell Computer Corporation onto a large screen in the front of the room. Wade assessed the trend and placed a trade on DELL with his broker. Within twenty minutes, Wade had made about $10,000 and had closed the trade with a second phone call without leaving the room. Wade was very impressive that morning. Unfortunately, I chose to hold onto my DELL options, feeling confident that "invincible" DELL would meet the analysts' expectations and make more impressive gains. The next day, February 11th, DELL continued its upward trend, and I caught a flight home from the conference feeling assured the trade would work out. The next morning, my broker phoned me to report that the trade had been stopped out at a loss. Almost in disbelief I asked why, and learned that two analysts from large brokerage firms had published concerns that DELL may slip in its percentage of revenue growth. The stock fell six points at the opening on February 12th, and another six points throughout the trading day. The market was closed February 15th for Presidents Day. On February 16th, DELL rebounded, recovering half the points it lost on the analysts' pre-announcement warning. After the market closed on February 16th, DELL posted earnings that actually beat the analysts' expectations. The company also announced a two-for-one stock split, but, as predicted, DELL missed a beat and posted slower annual revenue growth, a drop from 55%

to 38%. In spite of all the other positive news and announcements, the bad news regarding revenue growth slowing was enough to torpedo Dell and cause the price to sink lower.

Dell Computer Corporation is heavily traded and many investors lost money during this period. If they had known about Wade's quarterly-earnings, company-news pattern, however, they might have been able to take profits instead of losses. Let me explain why. Analyzing the quarterly-earnings pattern, the first thing you should notice is that the increase in newsy items prior to a company's quarterly earnings often produces a predictable up-trend prior to the posting date. So, if an investor knew when a company's quarterly period ended, he or she could take a position in the market and profit from the predictable uptrend. The last few days prior to the announcement itself, however, are dangerous, because that is the time analysts may issue warnings about the company, and their comments may cause the price to gap lower. With the announcement date still a few days away, an investor could lock in his or her profits from the uptrend by closing out early. That's what Wade did at the Semper Financial™ Convention in Los Angeles. He correctly assessed that DELL was in a significant uptrend, placed a short-term trade, and got out three days before the posting. He correctly anticipated that the days just before DELL's earnings announcement would be highly volatile and could cut both ways.

Summarizing, an investor should do his or her homework and know when a company's quarterly periods end, the day the company is likely to post earnings, and what the analysts are saying before an earnings announcement. He or she can't obtain the actual content of the report prior to the posting. That would be "insider information," which is regulated by the Securities and Exchange Commission. If it were allowed, "insider information" would give some traders an unfair advantage at the expense of others. So, the SEC requires companies to guard the contents of an earnings report with tight security. Without knowing the actual contents, an investor is betting on the possibilities, and hoping he or she has guessed the right way. Knowing these dates would enable the investor to enter the market four to six weeks ahead of the earnings report, take advantage of the predictable uptrend, and then sell the position one to three days before the actual announcement.

DOW JONES INDUSTRIALS

Wade's quarterly-earnings, company-news pattern functions more like a guideline than a rule. The difference is that guidelines apply to high probability outcomes and may be broken from time to time as outside elements interfere with the pattern. Rules, on the other hand, may not be broken without invalidating a principle. Examples from the Dow Jones Industrial 30 show how this works.

Allied Signal Inc. (ALD) closes its fiscal year on December 31st. The company last reported earnings on January 20, 1999. The analysts expected an earnings posting of 62¢ per share. ALD reported 63¢ a share, beating the estimates by 2.11%. Earnings rose 14% during the fourth quarter of 1998. One would expect a perfect correlation to the guideline with this example. It correlated, but not perfectly. About four weeks before the posting, ALD began a strong uptrend which ended prematurely during the first week in January, due largely to aviation industry sector problems that pulled ALD lower in sympathy. After the positive earnings posting on January 20 and a period of consolidation lasting about a week, the stock moved higher on strength.

Hewlett-Packard Company (HWP) closes its fiscal books on October 31st. The company reported earnings on November 16, 1998, and then again on February 16, 1999. The analysts' expected earnings of 75¢ a share in November and 83¢ a share in February. HWP reported

69¢ a share, disappointing the estimates by 7.75%. About six weeks before the posting, HWP began a surging uptrend which lasted until the earnings were reported on November 16th. After the disappointing report, HWP dropped sharply. Four weeks prior to the posting in February, HWP moved forward again anticipating the earnings report. The stock went to a new high, consolidated back, and surged forward until February 16th. This time HWP reported 95¢ earnings per share beating expectations by 15.01%.

The Walt Disney Company (DIS) closes its fiscal year on September 30th. The company reported earnings on November 3, 1998, and then again on January 27, 1999. The analysts expected earnings of 15¢ a share in November and 24¢ a share in February. DIS reported 14¢ a share in November, disappointing estimates by 7.89%. About four weeks before the posting, DIS began a surging uptrend which stalled on November 3rd. After the disappointing report, DIS traded sideways. Four weeks prior to the posting in January, DIS moved forward again, even gapping to a new high, anticipating the earnings report. This time DIS reported 30¢ a share earnings beating expectations by 25.52%. Even after this outstanding report, the stock consolidated and has been trading sideways since January 27th.

United Technologies Corporation (UTX) closes its fiscal books on December 31st. The company reported earnings on January 21st, 1999. The analysts expected earnings of $1.105 a share. UTX reported $1.23 a share beating the estimates by 11.31%. About four weeks before the posting, UTX began a surging uptrend which lasted until the earnings were reported. Since the posting, the company has continued to surge forward.

AT&T Corporation (T) closes its fiscal books on December 31st. The company reported earnings on January 25, 1999. The analysts expected earnings of $1.002 a share.

AT&T reported $1.140 a share beating the estimates by 13.77%. About six weeks before the posting, AT&T began a surging uptrend which lasted until the earnings were reported. After the positive report, AT&T continued uptrending for about one week and then dropped off, consolidating.

SUMMARY

All five split strategies – for options or stocks – play into the Red Light, Green Light timeline. You would do well to practice these entrance and exit points in conjunction with all available information.

In short, know your exit. Know why you're getting involved. The 'why' is just as important as the 'how.'

A man who knows how will always have a job. A man who knows why will always be the boss.

— DIANE RAVITCH

9

ARE YOU IN A RECESSION?

$\mathbf{M}$uch has happened this last year. "The old gray stock market ain't what it used to be" – sung to some catchy tune. I feel compelled to give an update to Volume 3 of my *Wall Street Money Machine* book series, originally titled *Bear Market Baloney*, now titled *Bulls and Bears* In this book, I stated that I did not see a bear market on the near horizon. That was 1998.

For more information on learning useful cash flow strategies and profiting in up or down markets, *Bulls and Bears, Wall Street Money Machine, Volume 3* is available in bookstores everywhere.

It is now 2001 and we have been in a rather mild recession since the early part of 2000, part of the problem extending back to the last half of 1999. Virtually all other contents of Volume 3, including the strategies and how to work them in a volatile market, still hold true. I, today, am of the same opinion.

The following is a selected excerpt from John F. Kennedy's Speech on December 14, 1962:

> *There are a number of ways by which the federal government can meet its responsibilities to aid economic growth. The most direct and significant kind of federal action aiding economic growth is to make possible an increase in private consumption and investment demand to cut the*

'fetters' which hold back private spending. In the past this could be done in part by the increased use of credit and monetary tools, but our balance of payments situation today places limits on our use of those tools for expansion. It could also be done by increasing federal expenditures more rapidly than necessary, but such a course would soon demoralize both the government and our economy. If government is to retain the confidence of the people, it must not spend more than can be justified on grounds of national need or spent with maximum efficiency. The final and best means of strengthening demand among consumers and business is to reduce the burden on private income and the deterrence to private initiative, which are imposed by our present tax system.

This administration pledged itself to an across-the-board top-to-bottom cut in personal and corporate income taxes to be enacted and become effective in 1963. I'm not talking about a quickie or a temporary tax cut, which would be more appropriate if a recession were imminent; nor am I talking about giving the economy a mere shot in the arm to ease some temporary complaint. I am talking about the accumulated evidence of the last five years that our present tax system, developed as it was in good part during World War II to restrain growth, exerts too heavy a drag on growth in peacetime:

- *It siphons out of the private economy too large a share of personal and business purchasing power.*

- *It also reduces the financial incentives for personal effort, investment, and risk-taking.*

In short, to increase demand and lift the economy, the federal government's most useful role is not to rush into a program of excessive increases in public expenditures, but to expand the incentives and opportunities for private expenditures.

Under these circumstances, any new tax legislation enacted, should meet the three following tests:

- First, it should reduce the net taxes by a sufficiently early date and a sufficiently large amount to do the job required.

  Early action could give us extra leverage, added results, and important insurance against recession. Too large a tax cut, of course, could result in inflation and insufficient future revenues – but the greater danger is a tax cut too little or too late to be effective.

- Second, the new tax bill must increase private consumption as well as investment.

  Corporate tax rates must also be cut to increase incentives and the availability of investment capital. The government has already taken major steps to reduce business tax liability and to stimulate the modernization, replacement, and expansion of our productive plant and equipment.

  Now we need to increase consumer demand to make these measures fully effective – demand which will make more use of existing capacity and thus increase both profits and the incentive to invest

- Third, the new tax bill should improve both the equity and the simplicity of our tax system.

  This means the enactment of long-needed tax reforms, a broadening of the tax base and the elimination or modification of many special tax privileges. These steps are not only needed to recover lost revenue and thus make possible a larger cut in present rates. They are also tied directly to our goal of greater growth. This inhibits our growth and efficiency as well as considerably complicating the work of both the taxpayer and the Internal Revenue Service. These various exclusions and concessions have been justified in the past as a means of overcoming the

*oppressively high rates in the upper brackets. A sharp re-
duction in those rates, accompanied by base-broadening,
loophole-closing measures, would properly make the new
rates not only lower but also more widely applicable.*

*Those are the three tests that the right kind of bill must
meet. And I am confident that the enactment of the right
bill next year will in due course increase our Gross National
Product by several times the amount of taxes actually cut.
Profit margins will be improved and both the incentive to
invest and the supply of internal funds for investment will
be increased. There will be new interest in taking risks.*

*Confidence in the dollar in the long run rests on confi-
dence in America, in our ability to meet our economic com-
mitments and reach our economic goals. In a world-wide
conviction that we are not drifting from recession to recession with no answer, the substantial improvement in our
balance of payments position makes it clear that nothing
could be more foolish than to restrict our growth merely to
minimize that particular problem because a slowdown in
our economy will feed that problem rather than diminish
it. European governmental and financial authorities have
urged us to cut taxes in order to expand our economy, attract more capital and increase confidence.*

*What concerns most Americans about a tax cut, I know,
is not the deficit in our balance of payments but the deficit
in our federal budget. Surely the lesson of the last decade
is that budget deficits are not caused by wild-eyed spend-
ers but by slow economic growth and periodic recessions,
and any new recession would break all deficit records. It is
a paradoxical truth that tax rates are too high today and
tax revenues are too low and the soundest way to raise
revenues in the long run is to cut rates now.*

*The purpose of cutting taxes is not to incur a budget
deficit, but to achieve the more prosperous, expanding
economy which will bring a budget surplus. I repeat: Our*

*practical choice is not between a tax-cut deficit and a bud-
getary surplus, it is between two kinds of deficits:*

1. *A chronic deficit of inertia, as the unwanted result
    of inadequate revenues.*

2. *A restricted economy, or a temporary deficit of tran-
    sition, resulting from a tax cut designed to boost
    the economy, increase tax revenue and achieve a
    future budget surplus – I believe this can be done.*

*The first type of deficit is a sign of waste and weak-
ness; the second reflects an investment in the future.*

*As the chairman of the House Ways and Means Com-
mittee pointed out, the size of the deficit is to be regarded
with concern and tax reduction must be accompanied, by
"increased control of the rises in expenditures." That is pre-
cisely the course we intend to follow.*

— JOHN F. KENNEDY

Now, let's move ahead about thirty-nine years. Here is a portion
of an article from *The Seattle Times* dated Saturday, March 10th, 2001:

*The market was smarting from a Labor Department report
that said 135,000 new jobs were created in February, ahead of
analysts' forecasts of about 75,000. The nation's unemployment
rate held steady at 4.2 percent.*

*The data, indicating increasing strength in the economy, might
relieve some pressure on the Federal Reserve to lower interest rates
to stimulate business activity.*

*Analysts said the market now expects the Fed to lower rates
by a quarter point, or perhaps not at all, when they meet March
20. Wall Street has been hoping for a half-point reduction.*

This last small recession seems to me to be a self-induced one.
We have talked ourselves into it. A recession occurs when leading
economic indicators go down two quarters in a row. We often don't
know a recession has occurred until after it's over, as it takes months

to gather certain data. Sometimes we're out of the recession or at least heading out of it before we know it has occurred.

Well, we've been in one, but the start of it, the duration and what it will take to get out of this one, are all quite different.

A bear market is a declining stock market, of say 20%, over a given period of time, about one year. Usually, bear markets follow recessions, or occur during them. This time, you'll see that this mini-bear market has preceded the recession. I might be so bold as to say that this bear market even caused this recession.

Let me explain. The bull market started by Ronald Reagan freeing up investment capital with his tax cuts and other economic policies, has run about eighteen years. It has had a few dips, but they have been minor. Even the crash of 1987 was over in about a year. I wrote extensively on that episode in my book on Gold Investing, called *Gold Rush* (Formerly *Y2K Gold Rush*).

Excerpted from *Gold Rush* is a short review of the recession, tax cut and the crash of 1987:

In the 1950s there were more paper dollars overseas than gold being held to back it up. Some European countries started converting their dollars back to gold – the price for gold went above $35 per oz. Free market economics were not dead.

In the mid 1960s, the LBJ "gang in charge" stopped minting silver coins. Why? The silver content was worth more than the face value of the coin. New coins with less silver were minted. What about the dollar?

In 1970, the dollar was still backed by a 25% gold storage. This 25% was eliminated. The dollar abroad was no longer redeemable in gold. The Nixon gang saw to that.

In the early years of the Nixon administration, several dark and devious things happened in the Democratic Congress.

With this latest debasing of the dollar, its value went plunging. Inflation worldwide was overheating. Stupidity now reigned supreme. Wages and price controls were imposed. What a low point for brainpower. Under President Ford and "Whip Inflation Now," the dollar continued to plunge. Carter's remedy (what remedy?) was a joke – money talks, but the action was worse.

In the late 1970s, a temporary good side effect occurred. Under Jimmy Carter (or with his help), the Federal Reserve Board raised the discount rate to the point that businesses could borrow from the private sector cheaper than borrowing from the Fed, and money poured back into the treasury.

With Reagan and his reduction in tax rates, the government took in more money. This was a huge outflow of dollars to other countries, and the dollar stopped its slide. But remember the piper (our U.S. debt, held by foreigners) had to be paid? Now a convergence of seemingly good things created a recession.

Let me explain: The dollar strengthened against other currencies; cheaper foreign goods flooded in; oil prices went way down and, in short, inflation died. Then bam, the recession of 1982 with an increase in unemployment off the charts.

By the end of the year the Fed once again lowered the discount rate – made credit easier, and the economy and the stock market took off.

A VIEW OF THE CRASH OF 1987
The years from the crash of 1929 to 1987 were very eventful for gold. In spite of the fact that Americans were not able to hold gold for over 40 of those years, gold was still a player in the world marketplace.

The government repealed the 50% tax on profits from silver. They also suspended the issuance of silver coins (the 90% silver content ones). Political uncertainty was everywhere, seen in the Second World War, the long and drawn out cold war, the division of Germany, Russian and Chinese expansionist policy, and the Vietnam War.

Toward the end of the 1970s, gold prices soared. This rapid increase, as mentioned elsewhere, was on the heels of double-digit inflation. Soon, however, in 1982, the prices on gold, silver, and platinum were way back down. Ironically, a long bull market commenced at this time. Precious metal prices, except for silver, rebounded to a higher level.

Then, one fine day in October 1987, the 19th to be exact, buying stocks stopped. Many people to this day have tried to fix blame on something. Here are a few of the bad guys:

1.   Foreigners quit buying our debt.

2.   Program trading was responsible.

3.   Overseas markets were overheated, then crashed. Many markets kept their doors closed.

4.   Tight money talk to curb inflation had been turned into higher rates for months (even years) preceding the crash. (By the way, I agree with this one.)

Whatever the cause, or grouping of causes, the specialists on the floor were without buyers. Computer brokers were not answering the phone. The market fell 508 points in one day. Option trading halted, stock index futures stopped trading.

Fear And Panic Spread

On Tuesday, with many exchanges closed, the Dow Jones Industrial Average fell another one hundred points and looked like it was headed for complete disaster, but lo and behold, it came back. The market (DJIA index – one of the only markets still trading), rallied.

A few things happened. Several companies announced they would be buying back their stock. This was positive, but nothing like what was going on behind the scenes.

To get the full impact of this, you have to realize how much buying is done with debt. Bank loans to major brokerage houses, margin investing had run rampant because of the bull market mentality – but now the collateral was gone.

The Fed came to the rescue. The Federal Reserve stepped in with billions of dollars to shore up the banks. Once those key players knew there was a safety net, the hemorrhaging stopped. The market bounced back. Within a year or so it was higher than before.

The lesson we've learned has a sad side effect. We know Uncle Sam is there. The corrections needed from time to time are dishonest. The price we pay is in the uncertainty about the true value of the market. We have some peace of mind knowing they will step in with cash and protect the market.

What can we do? (Several other chapters of *Gold Rush* deal with that.) Let me add two quick but powerful ending thoughts.

1. I've said it before; I'll say it a hundred times. We (that means you and me) need to stay on the gold standard: accumulate for emergencies, have enough to last a typical crisis – three months to two years – collect easily marketable coins, stay the course, don't despair. Make our life "as good as gold."

2. I don't want to get mushy here but there is a need to trust in God and keep our priorities right. Come what may, all will be well with us when we do good for God. Nations will come and go. Politicians will rise and fall. Bull and bear markets will be with us a long time. But through it all, we need to put God first, our families second, and the pursuit of wealth third. If the first two are correct, the last one will take care of itself.

> *Your gold and silver is cankered; and the rust of them*
> *shall be a witness against you, and shall eat your flesh as it*
> *were fire. Ye have heaped treasure together for the last days.*
> — JAMES 4:3

> *That the trial of your faith, being much more precious than of gold that perisheth, though it be tried with fire, might be found unto praise and honour and glory at the appearing of Jesus Christ.*
>
> — Peter 1:7

> *I counsel thee to buy of me gold tried in the fire, that thou mayest be rich; and white raiment, that thou mayest be clothed, and that the shame of thy nakedness do not appear; and anoint thine eyes with eyesalve, that thou mayest see.*
>
> — Revelation 3:18

Back to the here and now:

The bull market was strong. Even Clinton's policies couldn't stop it. Until something happened.

First, the capital markets exploded. Capital gains taxes, and personal income taxes brought out the investors in droves. Companies had easy access to money. Almost too easy. In 1991, the Internet hit the consciousness of most Americans. By 1993 companies on the Internet exploded. They were everywhere. The dot.coms.

Like always, companies servicing the Internet did well – like selling picks and shovels during the gold rush of 1847. Revenues grew into the billions. Profits soared. But nothing soared as much as the stock prices.

Ironically, the Internet provided easy access to information, including systems for personal investing, and opportunities for ownership in these same companies. Everyone was betting on the future. Dubious companies with weak business plans were driven up to billions of dollars. The air got thin.

Then the government got involved. The Fed, in its never-ending quest to curb inflation, saw the new enemy, the cause of the new inflation were these high-priced stocks. Usually they raised the discount rate (and put out other predictions) to showdown inflation. This time, they raised the rates to slow down the stock market.

Ironically, it was the worst thing they could have done. Think of it. At a time when companies ran out of investor's money, and would then turn

AMAZON.COM

ANERICA ONLINE

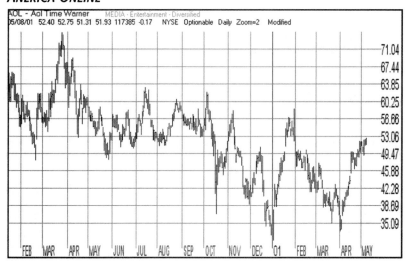

DELL COMPUTERS

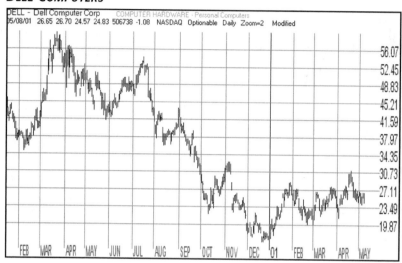

LUCENT TECHNOLOGIES

ORACLE CORPORATION

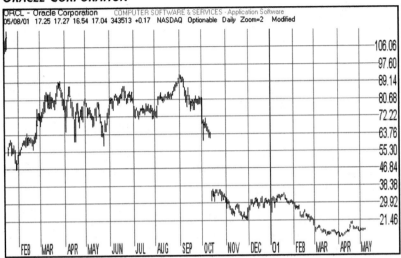

SUN MICROSYSTEMS

to more traditional sources (with more checks and balances), they dried up the money. They should have lowered rates to help more economic expansion and then maybe some of these companies' earnings would have caught up with their stock prices.

Like a San Francisco chase scene, the fall was great. On the way down, they hit and hurt a lot of other companies.

Even great companies saw the economic expansion stalling and cut back. Now, dot.coms and other computer people were out of work. Jobs, though available, were tougher to find. Companies could be more selective.

Great companies have even slowed down. Some are still growing, but the rate of growth is not as robust. Their stocks got hammered. Look at the following charts courtesy of Bloomberg:

Talk is cheap. Stock market news TV coverage also started up and you know how they thrive on negative news. The Red Light, Green Light phenomena I've written about still works. In fact, it's more important now than ever to understand these forces which drive the market, and today these forces have accomplices in the media.

The adage to "buy on rumor, sell on news," sure seems to play out almost daily in the stock market. It seems that anticipation moves the market, and little else. Oh, I know good or bad news is important, but often times I feel the play is over before the actual news hits the streets. It's news to us little guys, but two days old to the big players. They seem to make their living being one step ahead of the pack.

The updates on W.I.N. included in this book, have been fun and entertaining. It's now March 13, 2001. Yesterday the DOW dipped over four hundred points. It was an awful day. It's now in two weeks from 10,900 to now just over 10,000. When it was 10,400+, I said I thought it would go up to 10,800, maybe 10,900 and then possibly bump against 11,000. I also said it doesn't have legs. It cannot be sustained. I repeated that there is too much negative sentiment in the market and too many corporations bad-mouthing their futures. WHAM! Intel, Cisco and others did just that.

We're also still in a major economic Red Light period. We need a rush of good news and we may not get it.

Then, retail sales numbers came in. In general, the numbers were slightly up. But now, let's try to get into the head of the media, or the major players. How will this be perceived? The main question, sadly, focuses on the Fed meeting on March 20th.

A brief update. Many of us have thought, or at least hoped, the Fed would lower the discount rate. There was a brief rally in January when the Fed unexpectedly lowered the rate. No meeting, no preview, just wham, out of the blue they dropped the rate – big time. The market reacted nicely, but it was short-lived.

Here is the actual Federal Reserve news release:

Release Date: January 3, 2001

For immediate release: The Federal Open Market Committee decided today to lower its target for the federal funds rate by 50 basis points to 6 percent.

In a related action, the Board of Governors approved a 25-basis-point decrease in the discount rate to 5-3/4 percent, the level requested by seven Reserve Banks. The Board also indicated that it stands ready to approve a further reduction of 25 basis points in the discount rate to 5-1/2 percent on the requests of Federal Reserve Banks.

These actions were taken in light of further weakening of sales and production, and in the context of lower consumer confidence, tight conditions in some segments of financial markets, and high energy prices sapping household and business purchasing power. Moreover, inflation pressures remain contained. Nonetheless, to date there is little evidence to suggest that longer-term advances in technology and associated gains in productivity are abating.

The Committee continues to believe that, against the background of its long-run goals of price stability and sustainable economic growth and of the information currently available, the risks are weighted mainly toward conditions that may generate eco-nomic weakness in the foreseeable future.

In taking the discount rate action, the Federal Reserve Board approved requests submitted by the Boards of Directors of the Federal Reserve Banks of New York, Cleveland, Atlanta, St. Louis, Kansas City, Dallas and San Francisco.

Anticipation. You're probably tired of hearing this, but, "The current price of stock (in the open auction we call the stock market) is based on the anticipation of future earnings." Everything, and I mean everything, is important to this. Sales, debt, mergers, layoffs, lawsuits, earnings, new products, spin-offs, buyouts, share buy backs, stock splits, dividend increases and decreases, added to list (index) or delisted – and many, many more.

Obviously, each event is not as important as the next one. Some news events play out quickly, some live longer. Some good news events of a particular company may be overwhelmed by other bad news in the marketplace, and vice versa.

The question: What is more important: the actual news, or the anticipation – even rumors – that drive stocks up a little more? Another point: "anticipation" and "rumors" are a little bit longer lived than actual news events–say a press conference and then within hours or overnight the news has played out.

Look at this chart and we'll then get back to the retail earnings report:

DOW JONES INDUSTRIAL AVERAGE

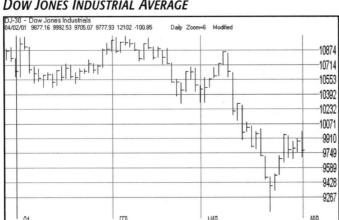

The market tanked yesterday – again on certain big company "bigwigs" saying ugly futuristic things about their revenue or earnings: Intel, Cisco and others. Jeff Besos of Amazon.com in Europe said he wouldn't invest in Internet stocks right now. He should just be quiet.

These excerpts are off the wires of Bloomberg:

MONDAY, MARCH 13, 2001 6:29
CISCO SYSTEMS, INC. (CSCO):
Chief Executive Jeff Chambers said the maker of equipment to link computers isn't seeing turnaround in spending by phone companies and is considering a share buyback. Chambers made his comments in a presentation at the Merrill Lynch Global Communications Investors Conference in New York. Cisco fell $1.81 to $18.81

CISCO SYSTEMS INC.

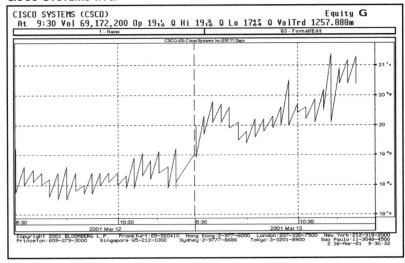

MONDAY MARCH 13, 2001 8:22
CISCO SYSTEMS, INC. (CSCO):
Chief Executive John Chambers said spending by smaller U.S. phone companies is "stabilizing" after a steep drop that caused a slowdown in equipment sales.

Phone companies and large corporations cut spending plans for networking gear in the past three quarters, forcing Cisco, Nortel Networks Corp.

and other equipment suppliers to cut forecasts. On Feb. 6, Cisco said it expects sales in the fiscal third quarter ending April, to be "flat to down 5%" compared with the previous period.

"It looks like it's beginning to stabilize off of that very low base." Chambers said in a presentation at the Merrill Lynch Global Communications Investors Conference in New York. He didn't identify any Cisco customers.

Cisco had more than quadrupled sales in the past four years largely by selling to the smaller phone companies known as competitive local-exchange carriers.

Here is Cisco's two-day chart:

This morning, the man from Intel said some bullish things. The stock was down yesterday (March 12th) on the bad forecasts, but up today on his statements.

What about the marketplace in general? When the news played out – the first decrease in the Fed rate – the market went up. Then, all kinds of other, more bullish news hit the streets. Housing starts are up; yes, the dot.coms are pulling back, but unemployment has not risen; things are not that bad – *all of this* – had everyone believing the Federal Reserve Board would not lower the rates. That's the primary reason the market slid – plus, this market is in a February (typical) Red Light period. We need to get to the second half of March.

Today, even though the retail numbers are up, they're not up enough. The market, once again, feels like rates might be lowered. It bottoms out and starts to back up. I bought the $100 calls and the $106 calls on the DJX – this represents the DJIA 30 at 10,000 and 10,600. I'm bullish for the near-term.

Watch the results on WIN. Just for fun, I'll put the January 31, 2001 Press Release in here, so you can get a feel for how this looks and feels.

For Immediate Release: January 31, 2001:

The Federal Open Market Committee at its meeting today decided to lower its target for the federal funds rate by 50 basis points to 5-1/2 percent. In a related action, the Board of Gover-

nors approved a 50 basis point reduction in the discount rate to 5 percent.

Consumer and business confidence has eroded further, exacerbated by rising energy costs that continue to drain consumer purchasing power and press on business profit margins. Partly as a consequence, retail sales and business spending on capital equipment have weakened appreciably. In response, manufacturing production has been cut back sharply, with new technologies appearing to have accelerated the response of production and demand to potential excesses in the stock of inventories and capital equipment.

Taken together, and with inflation contained, these circumstances have called for a rapid and forceful response of monetary policy. The longer-term advances in technology and accompanying gains in productivity, however, exhibit few signs of abating and these gains, along with the lower interest rates, should support growth of the economy over time.

Nonetheless, the Committee continues to believe that against the background of its long-run goals of price stability and sustainable economic growth and of the information currently available, the risks are weighted mainly toward conditions that may generate economic weakness in the foreseeable future.

In taking the discount rate action, the Federal Reserve Board approved requests submitted by the Boards of Directors of the Federal Reserve Banks of New York, Philadelphia, Cleveland, Atlanta, Chicago, St. Louis, Minneapolis, Dallas and San Francisco.

WHAT NOW?

We need good earnings announcements. We need bounces. The interest rates will be lowered. The good news will start on schedule. We need the Bears to carry the day, and they have. The Bulls are temporarily gone. That's good.

I also see a caution – yea, yea, yea, and people starting to question; to look harder at companies. Before there can be a flight to quality stocks, there has to be a flight to quality thinking.

The market will muddle along. It's a perfect market (rolling with an upward line) for Wade Cook type cash flow strategies. Let's go!

EARLY MARKET UPDATE

As I write this, the days are passing away as we head to the green light period, which starts about March 15 – at least, for companies with good news.

I see a phenomenon that bears observing. I'll do my best to explain and try to connect the dots for you. I see the market place sloughing off bad news. A few days ago there were more serious downgrades on an index of high-tech stocks, many rose in price. Weird. A few earnings forecast to the negative caused a few ripples, then the stocks rose. The market seems to want to go up. TV commentators are having a tough time, they can't explain it. I can. We had a vastly overpriced grouping of stocks. We had a correction. Now, people are more careful. Also, we're entering a news-reporting season and it just feels like the market, or at least certain stocks, want to rise. However, as of right now, the market had no legs.

Until lower interest rates take effect and until the Bush tax reduction of rates takes hold, the market will move sideways. This is perfect for Red Light, Green Light enthusiasts.

The following are selected excerpts from my book *Wall Street Money Machine: Volume 3, Bulls and Bears* and will help you to understand a bear or a bull market.

There are countless people who do not know what a bull or a bear market is. They have been through both, but don't even know it. These people do not know how to play the ups and downs. This gives my company and me a great opportunity for service.

Even in a bear market, you can still be profitable and employ the money machine concepts.

You can tell the signs of a bear market before they happen. Think about it. If a bear market (however short and insignificant) is caused by certain factors: high interest rates (which could have occurred by a Fed worrying about inflation and which could end with lower corporate earnings occurring simultaneously, or close to each other), high taxes, high inflation, and low corporate earnings; and if a bull market is caused by the opposite (low interest rates, relatively low taxes, lower inflation, and good earnings), then the answer is simple: watch for real moves – up or down – in these areas. I say real because the Fed might tinker with the rates in response to fears (not actual occurrences) of things that they think are important.

> *It isn't as important to buy as cheap as possible as it is to buy at the right time.*
>
> — Jesse Livermore

Let's define a bear market: A bear market could be anything from nine months to two years of a downturn in the market. How much of a percentage of a downturn you may ask? You can expect to see a 20% to 30% drop in the total equities in the DOW, or even in the Standard and Poors 500 (S&P 500), or in the NASDAQ. And if the market turns down in even a one or two month period of time, this does not constitute a bear market.

For example, the Dow went from 9,400 in the summer 1998, then dropped to 7,500 and then is over 10,000 in just a few months period of time. Because the market is always fluctuating, you're going to have those little ups and downs and you may have a month when it slides off a few points. The downward trend has to be sustained to be considered a bear market.

What causes a bear market? There can be a number of factors. Here are three main causes:

1. Bad corporate earnings,

2. Higher inflation, and

3. High interest rates.

In my stock market seminars, I encourage people not to slip into a bear market mentality. Just because we enter a bear market does not mean all is lost. We can fight back. We can prepare. Our choices are varied and have profound consequences. One option is to sit out an overall bear market. The second part we'll deal with stocks which act like they're in a bear market, even though we're in a bull market.

DOWN MARKET STOCKS

Just because we enter a bear market does not mean that every stock goes down – or goes down dramatically. Some are recession-proof and some even fare very well. I'll make three general comments about finding good stocks in down markets.

1. *News articles,* more specifically, magazine articles, are loaded with information about companies which fare well, or have fared well, in down markets.

2. *There are a few firms that analyze stocks.* Some overanalyze. Many stocks actually buck the trend of a downturn. These stocks are said to be "negative beta down" by the "techies." The beta of a stock is a measuring tool to see the volatility of a stock, or the likelihood of price changes, as measured against the movement in price of the underlying stocks. There is also a beta of stock as compared to the S&P 500. For example; if a stock has a beta of 1.2, it is said to be 0.2 or 20% more volatile that the S&P. A beta of 2 would be a high flying, very volatile stock with a huge 2x increase compared to the norm. A negative beta, say 0.8, is 20% less volatile the norm of 1. The model can get more sophisticated. The analysis of "negative beta down" is extensive. This information is valuable, if one is looking for stocks with good potential during down markets.

3. *Good charting services* can help you track stock performances, measure movements, or buying power. You should subscribe to one of these services for current information.

UP MARKET STOCKS

In a bull market, many stocks do poorly. Some for no apparent reason whatsoever. Big dips just happen. Maybe because of program buying or selling. Maybe bad news (buying out the short sellers). Maybe competition. Sometimes the events are unexplainable; sometimes they're not.

Here are two major points I'd like to make:

1. In up and down markets there are exceptions to the rule, or in other words, stocks that underperform or outperform the norm. It is finding these oddball stocks and either ignoring them or figuring out how to play them, which can make us money.

2. There are specific formulas, or methods, which can be employed to make money in any market. In down markets (this usually means flat market after a serious decrease in value) there are companies which excel. Yes, it's tough to buck the trend, but well managed companies not only do better, but they attract investors like a powerful magnet. The law of supply and demand takes hold and you have buyers choosing a few good stocks, driving the price up.

For precise and effective stock market trading, it is difficult to express the importance of working within the Red Light, Green Light format. News, the quality and quantity, or the lack thereof, is too essential a series of events to ignore. Indeed, to truly grasp the movement of stocks and get your money in front of the news, or out of the way of no-news can make a difference in your cash flow of tens of thousands of dollars per year. These movements can spell disaster or success.

10

YOUR PERSONAL LIFE

I often use the Bible to make my point. I have created a series of Special Reports, *Soar With Eagles*, that are dedicated to specific Bible topics. Below is an excerpt from Special Report #700, the Preface of the *Soar With Eagles* Series. This particular report deals with the wisdom that comes while acquiring knowledge. Seeking information for the purpose of wise application of that knowledge can be the means of bringing about all good things in life.

Do you realize that a common use of the word "wisdom" meant a collection of knowledge that could be searched out and understood? Sages and wisdom practitioners spent their lives learning, discussing and then teaching this "gained wisdom" to others.

Man, to some degree, has always attributed the workings of the world to God. Many beliefs, based on true principles, were nevertheless corrupted as these sages interposed their own beliefs on the philosophy of God. One major shift was that a particular God ruled many things in nature. There was a God of the wind; a God of the water; a God of War; a God of Love. The Chaldeans, the Egyptians; later the Greeks and many others believed this way. Abraham was well-versed in these teachings. A big part of this theosophy (or theology) was the movement of the stars. The sages found work in interpreting these events of nature. They also studied numbers and were big into interpreting dreams.

Abraham, though, learned of and then worshiped the one true God. He was to put aside such beliefs and worship God, the Creator. God the undivided one. He was to leave his home in Ur and travel. He found a home in Haran, but was told to move on. He finally settled where God wanted him in what is now Canaan. Abraham was the first Hebrew. "Hebrew" means "wanderer" or "sojourner."

God established His covenant with Abraham. I've written extensively on this in *Business Buy the Bible*, and ask you to go there. At least read Genesis 17:7-9. Through Abraham's sons and all of his posterity the world will be blessed.

Let's use Job, chapter 28 for our study text. First of all, a word about Job. Job lived long before Abraham. He was not a Hebrew. He believed in the one true God. To the sages of the time, everything had to make sense. If it did not it was chalked up as a mystery. Many of these sages sought God in natural phenomena.

The basic rule was that of cause and effect. The other gods wanted you to live a certain way. If you did, they would be pleased and bless you. Negative actions, conversely, brought about negative consequences. In short, the god of the wind will blow your house down if you sin. Job was much different than these other sages who were tucked away debating in the more civilized centers of the world.

I've written about Job from several different angles. See *Business Buy the Bible*, Chapter 5 and *Soar With Eagles*, reports #708 and #712. Job is part of the collection of wisdom literature that I have used so frequently, and while the word "wisdom" is often used in Job to refer to discernment and understanding – the "to get it" viewpoint – wisdom is also used to mean knowledge – again, and especially, that collection of facts, information and knowledge known by the sages to understand their world and try to understand God. Let's look at part of chapter 28 in the book of Job.

People had knowledge of certain things. They knew how to find in the earth gold and silver. They knew how to heat rocks and extract metals (verse 2). They knew somewhat of floods, rains, seasons. They knew how to harvest grains and make bread (verse 5).

They knew many things of the earth, but they did not know it all. In verse 22 it says he, meaning God, knows all. "...and the thing that is hid bringeth he forth to light."

Then Job goes on with a question:

> *But where shall wisdom be found? And where is the place of understanding? It can't be bought at any price. It can't be found in the usual places. It is to be found in the "fear of the Lord."*
>
> — JOB 28:28

SKILLFUL KNOWLEDGE

We should also think of wisdom as a description and reference to skillful use of knowledge, and find great insights in Exodus. Moses was about to build the tabernacle, a place for the Ark of the Covenant, in the wilderness. First, offerings were needed.

> *Take ye from among you an offering unto the Lord: whosoever is of a willing heart...*
>
> — EXODUS 35:5

Knowledge of specific skills was needed.

> *And every wise hearted among you shall come, and make all that the Lord hath commanded.*
>
> — EXODUS 35:10

> *And they came, both men and women, as many as were willing hearted...*
>
> — EXODUS 35:22

> *And he hath filled him with the spirit of God, in wisdom, in understanding, and in knowledge, and in all manner of workmanship;*
>
> — EXODUS 35:31

Them hath he filled with wisdom of heart, to work all manner of work, of the engraver, and of the cunning workman, and of the embroiderer, in blue, and in purple, in scarlet and in fine linen, and of the weaver, even of them that do any work, and of those that devise cunning work.

— EXODUS 35:36

"Cunning" here means skillful, or a skilled workmanship.

The point I'm trying to make is that knowledge for knowledge's sake is important. Think about the wisdom of Solomon. You see, Solomon's wisdom stood out, because David's kingdom, all of Israel, was on the periphery of the philosophical wisdom centers of Greece, Babylon and Egypt. Israel was "out in the boondocks." In fact, the only person said to be wise among Israel's descendants was Joseph.

After the verses that mentioned Solomon's wisdom and how great his wisdom was, it goes on to list how many Psalms and verses he knew. But then the following is added:

And he spake of trees, from the cedar tree that is in Lebanon even unto the hyssop that springeth out of the wall: he spake also of beasts, and of fowl, and of creeping things, and of fishes. And there came of all people to hear the wisdom of Solomon, from all kings of the earth, which had heard of his wisdom.

— I KINGS 4:33:34

Simply put, Solomon knew things. Again, wisdom here is a knowledge of things.

PREDICTIONS OR PROJECTIONS?

All of the information and wisdom we have must be applied so as to make a difference in our lives. Here are a few thoughts:

1. Wisdom is knowledge, but finds fruition as it is acted upon. Wisdom could be as simple as using a stepladder to reach a dish off a high shelf, or figuring out how to set your VCR. The principle use of wisdom is to show us how to live properly.

> *One should ask for wisdom above all other virtues, for it contains everything else.*
>
> RABBI SIMEON BEN HALAFTA

2. You must learn the limits of wisdom. For example, our physical bodies can only do so much. We speak to teach, but the listener hears not. Our minds can also only handle so much.

> *So teach us to number our days, that we may apply our hearts unto wisdom.*
>
> — PSALM 90:12

3. We need to learn when to speak and when to be quiet.

> *Teach wisdom to one who knows not, and learn from one who knows. By doing this you will know what you do not know and remember what you indeed know.*
>
> — SOLOMON IBN GABIROL

4. Learn wisdom from wise people. Men and women, in their own ways, have special insights. Wisdom can be learned in relationships, and not only learned, but applied and enlarged.

5. When human wisdom runs out, we can always turn to God. How comforting.

> *God understandeth the way...*   — JOB 28:23

> *For the Lord giveth wisdom: out of his mouth cometh knowledge and understanding.*
>
> — PROVERBS 2:6

> *Wisdom constantly receives influence from above and gives spirituality below.*
>
> NEWMAN IN THE HASIDIC ANTHOLOGY

One appropriate way to view wisdom is to figure out the affect(s) of the cause(s); ie: seeing future results from current actions. The key here is to "figure things out," and then make better choices. *It is not about predicting outcomes, but about projecting outcomes.*

For precise and effective stock market trading, it is difficult to express the importance of working within the Red Light, Green Light format. News, the quality and quantity, or lack thereof, is too essential a series of events to ignore. Indeed, to truly grasp the movement of stocks and then get your money in front of the news, or out of the way of no-news can make a difference in your cash flow of tens of thousands of dollars per year. These movements can spell disaster *or* success.

What about news in the spiritual side of our life? How big of a difference would there be in our life if we do or do not receive regular "updates" in the area of spiritual well-being? I know this is a jump to go from the stock market to church, but what if we "gain the whole world and lose our souls?" Because the spiritual side of life is so very important to me, I'll risk offending some and bring these ideas up anyway.

Our emotions, the spiritual quality of our life, can have red light periods if we let it. We can, by not surrounding ourselves with good news, be in a downtrend just like our favorite stock. We need news, we need awareness, and we need motivation, both external and internal. We will wither on the vine without it.

Try this on for size: from ancient times God's word has been to rest, to spiritually recuperate, and give one day to Him. That's every seventh day, or shabbat – The Sabbath. He knows best for us and wants us to have *at least* a weekly spiritual feeding.

Stocks need (or get) news every five to six weeks. The news is sometimes good, sometimes bad. In our own lives, we virtually need *daily* news – the good news being the Gospel. This news is always good, even when everything else around us has turned bad. We should at least fill up our tanks weekly with the appropriate fuel to keep us going "in the way."

For example, the messages in the Bible are wonderful, uplifting and consistent. We cannot think that we can go to church once a year and be spiritually prepared to "take on the world." We are deluding ourselves if we think so.

> *We are of the ruminating kind, and it is not enough to cram ourselves with a great load of collections. Unless we chew them over again, they will not give us strength and nourishment.*
>
> — CHANNING

Our brains – the rationalization and excuses put forth – get us into a lot of trouble when we think we're smarter than God. Our Church should not be the ways of the world. Our Bible should not be the front page of the newspaper, nor our Sermons the six o'clock news. Our thinking process should not start with "what can I get out of anything and everything?"

> *For my thoughts are not your thoughts, neither are your ways my ways, saith the Lord. For as the heavens are higher than the earth, so are my ways higher than your ways, and my thoughts than your thoughts.*
>
> — ISAIAH 55:8-9

> *O God, our Father, we pray that the people of America, who have made such progress in material things, may now seek to grow in spiritual understanding.*
>
> *For we have improved means, but not improved ends. We have better ways of getting there, but we have no better places to go. We can save more time, but are not making any better use of the time we save.*
>
> *We need Thy help to do something about the world's true problems – the problem of lying, which is called propaganda; the problem of selfishness, which is called self-interest; the problem of greed, which is often called profit; the problem of license, disguising itself as liberty; the problem of lust, masquerading as love; the problem of*

materialism, the hook which is baited with security.

Hear our prayers, O Lord, for the spiritual understanding which is better than political wisdom, that we may see our problems for what they are. This we ask in Jesus' name. Amen.

— PETER MARSHALL

If we do not amend our ways, our life could be like a long, giant, Red Light period. How sad that would be, yet how easy to rectify!

These insights, these spiritual news flashes, can come from many different directions. We find them in good books (including Scriptures), through prayer, in music and in daily conversations. We can tune our senses to receive this good news whenever and wherever it shows up. We can actively seek the news that brings positive changes to our lives, and gives us the green light for continued growth and joy in living.

I'm confident God wants to keep giving us His Good News, we need it more often than we think. You need never again go into a spiritual Red Light period. Get your personal board of directors to vote for this kind of life. Then, get your corporate officers – that's you: you're the President, Vice President, Secretary and Treasurer of your life – to stay in the Green Light area.

We came from someplace and we're going someplace. So, we should make our time here an exciting adventure. The architect of the universe didn't build a stairway leading nowhere.

— GROVE PATTERSON, TOLEDO DAILY

Appendix

AVAILABLE **R**ESOURCES

The following books, videos, and audiocassettes have been reviewed by the Stock Market Institute of Learning™, Lighthouse Publishing Group, Inc., or Gold Leaf Press staff and are suggested as reading and resource material for continuing education to help with your financial planning, and real estate and stock market trading. Because new ideas and techniques come along and laws change, we're always updating our products.

To order a copy of our current catalog, please write or call us at:

Stock Market Institute of Learning, Inc.™
14675 Interurban Avenue South
Seattle, Washington 98168-7411
1-800-872-7411

Or visit us on our web sites at:

www.smil-inc.com
www.Lighthousebooks.com
www.upwego.com

Also, we would love to hear your comments on our products and services, as well as your testimonials on how these products have benefited you. We look forward to hearing from you!

AUDIOCASSETTES

THE FINANCIAL FORTRESS HOME STUDY COURSE
PRESENTED BY WADE B. COOK

This eight-part series is the last word in entity structuring. It goes far beyond mere financial planning or estate planning. It helps you to structure your business and affairs so that you can avoid the majority of taxes, retire rich, escape lawsuits, bequeath your assets to your heirs without government interference, and, in short, bomb-proof your entire estate. There are six audiocassette seminars on tape, an entity structuring video, and a full kit of documents.

POWER OF NEVADA CORPORATIONS — A FREE CASSETTE
PRESENTED BY WADE B. COOK

Nevada Corporations have secrecy, privacy, minimal taxes, no reciprocity with the IRS, and protection for shareholders, officers, and directors. This is a powerful seminar.

SAIL: SCRIPTURAL APPLICATIONS IN LIFE
PRESENTED BY WADE B. COOK

In this day and age, the separation between money matters and spiritual matters seem to be drifting apart. Bring God and the Bible back into your daily business life. Introducing a most fascinating look at the business of life, by *New York Times* best-selling author Wade Cook. This set contains powerful lessons on setting your priorities and how to apply them in your every day life. This is the first of three enlightening discussions about applying age-old principles to your daily life, principles that can affect your spiritual as well as your financial well being. Wade Cook calls this his "Sail Through Life" seminar. This important discussion deals with questions like: How does your desire to increase your wealth sit with your maker? What kinds of feelings to you think God has about your profiting in the stock market? Do you think that God wants you to be rich? Wade uses the scriptures to show examples in history of how God blessed his people with wealth and riches. Wealth is neutral. It's what we do with it that's important.

AUDIO COMPACT DISCS

Zero To Zillions™
Presented by Wade B. Cook

Zero to Zillions is an easy-to-follow, easy-to-understand, and teaches easy-to-implement methods and techniques designed for consistent cash flow from the stock market. This mega course on stock market income formulas is taught in a lively format of real examples, great expectations, functional demonstrations and presentations. Zero to Zillions has beautiful filled-in manuals (notes taken as if you were in the live events) with documentation, examples and add-on materials.

Financial Fortress Audio Series
Presented by Wade B. Cook

Protection of your family and assets is key if you want a comfortable and secure future. Now you can learn the financial structuring strategies taught at the Wealth Institute™ in the comfort of your own home or in your car. Now is the time to listen to the Financial Fortress audiotape set: Learn to achieve optimum growth and protection of your personal and business assets. Protect yourself and your business from the burden of ever–increasing federal and state taxes, and from frivolous lawsuits. Create a comfortable retirement for yourself and your family. Learn to avoid probate. All of this entity structuring information is put together onto six audiotape sets and packaged together with: the Entity Integration Video, the Incorporation Handbook, the Brilliant Deductions Manual and the Documents and Forms Kit. The Financial Fortress is a great way to reinforce what you learned at the Wealth Institute! Learn to increase your cash flow, slash your taxes and bombproof your assets from lawsuits.

13 Fantastic Income Formulas – A Free Compact Disc
Presented by Wade B. Cook

Learn thirteen cash flow formulas, some of which are taught in the Wall Street Workshop™. Learn to double some of your money in $2^1/_2$ to 4 months.

3/8 TO WEALTH
PRESENTED DARLENE NELSON

Designed to help teach and dramatically improve trading skills, select better candidates, and learn and incredible repeatable system for success that has put many of our students ahead of the pack. Never trade in the dark again. Trade with confidence knowing exactly which stocks and options you will trade the next day if the trade presents itself.

MARKET AIKIDO
PRESENTED BY RYAN LITCHFIELD

Developed by Ryan Litchfield, Market Aikido is a unique insight into the mandatory mindset of successful trading. Becoming a trader can be very profitable but it can also be the most difficult thing you ever learn. Aikido is a beautiful martial art that is all about defense, counter move and conflict resolution. Market Aikido shows you how your emotions are triggered and how and why you have so little control of your response. The lessons of Aikido help you lower the pressure of trading and reveals the origins of bad trading habits.

POOLSIDE INVESTING WITH LEAPS®
PRESENTED BY DARLENE NELSON

This course is designed to power profits in a busy lifestyle. Trade in 2-5 hours a month without intense market involvement. Learn the ins and outs of trading with LEAPs and understand how LEAPs can be traded utilizing secrets that only Darlene Nelson can expose.

STOCK SPLIT SECRETS
PRESENTED BY DARLENE NELSON

This incredible course was designed to let you in on the secrets of BIG MONEY PLAYERS. Stock splits have predictable patterns that can enhance earnings. Learn when to get in and out for potentially big time profits. No matter what strategy you decide to trade, if you learn the power and secrets of stock splits you will enhance your trading style.

BOOKS AND SPECIAL REPORTS

WALL STREET MONEY MACHINE
WALL STREET MONEY MACHINE SERIES, VOLUME 1
WRITTEN BY WADE B. COOK

This revised and updated version of the book that appeared on the *New York Times* Business Best Sellers list for over one year is all about revolutionary cash-flow strategies – monthly checks you put in the bank. In this volume, Wade Cook introduces you to the Money Machine and Meter Drop™ way of putting your money to work. Wade's dynamic and innovative, yet simple to understand and easy to implement methods will get you on the road to wealth – how to build it, how to enhance it, how to protect it, and how to keep it growing. You work hard for your money – now get your money working hard for you. Get your own *Wall Street Money Machine* started today!

STOCK MARKET MIRACLES
WALL STREET MONEY MACHINE SERIES, VOLUME 2
WRITTEN BY WADE B. COOK

Finally! A book by an author that understands what the average investor needs: knowing when to sell. The information in this book will give you the ability to make money using real tried-and-true techniques. No special knowledge required, no strings attached. These tools can help you secure real wealth. Thanks to Wade Cook, financial miracles happen every day for thousands of students who are applying what they learned from this book. Create some miracles in your life!

BULLS & BEARS
WALL STREET MONEY MACHINE SERIES, VOLUME 3
WRITTEN BY WADE B. COOK

This volume is dedicated to the concept of a bear market – not how to avoid one, but how to make money when the market is going down! Harness the hysteria that drives the market, and take advantage of the valleys and peaks that constantly occur. Learn how to be a better participant in the market by being a better observer of the market: both as a student and as a trader. You can ride the waves and reap profits in any kind of market. If you've been scared by the headlines, learn how to prosper in the coming years, even in a bear market!

SAFETY 1ST INVESTING
WALL STREET MONEY MACHINE SERIES, VOLUME 4
Written by Wade B. Cook

For most investors, safe investing means low returns. Why follow the advisors who only give you one investment strategy – buy and hold. Now learn to maximize your returns while you minimize your risk! Safety in real estate, safety in business, and safety in the stock market has to have as a core objective the preservation of capital. Assets need to increase in value, not decrease. Even before we grow our assets, we must figure out how not to lose value. Simply put, the first strategy in winning is to not lose. Get your money out of the way of danger, and get it in the way of progress.

FREE STOCKS
WALL STREET MONEY MACHINE SERIES, VOLUME 5
WRITTEN BY WADE B. COOK

FREE! The word and concept have been the advertising foundation for billion dollar corporations, the heartbeat of huge marketing campaigns, and the nexus between companies and customers for eons. Now Wade Cook introduces the LOCC™ (Large Option Covered Calls™) system -- a strategy that has generated 80% to 100% returns on some trades using margin in the year 2000. If you like the buy-and-hold strategy of investing, how do you get the money to pay for your stock? Wade Cook demonstrates how to get the market to pay for your stock with five to seven months using his new LOCC™ system. Learn how to start building the portfolio of your dreams -- for FREE!

STOCK SPLIT SECRETS™: PROFITING FROM A POWERFUL, PREDICTABLE PRICE-MOVING EVENT
WRITTEN BY MILES AND DARLENE NELSON

This book is about making phenomenal money in the stock market! If you have a desire to trade in the stock market, this book is your ticket to success. Witty, fun, comprehensive, and a must read for anyone building wealth – no matter what trading or investing strategy you use now, or plan to use in the future. You can dramatically increase your earnings by adding the power of stock splits. Renowned authors and speaking team Miles and Darlene Nelson share their secrets in this easy to read, information-packed book. They reveal how they profit and earn their living trading in the stock market. The definitive guide to investing and trading companies that split their stock, it extensively covers the basics and offers finesse formulas for seasoned traders. Because of its unique writing style, *Stock Split Secrets* appeals to seasoned veterans and supercharges beginner investors.

101 WAYS TO BUY REAL ESTATE WITHOUT CASH
WRITTEN BY WADE B. COOK

Wade Cook has personally achieved success after success in real estate. This book fills the gap left by other authors who have given all the ingredients for real estate investing, but not the whole recipe. This is the book for the investor who wants innovative and practical methods for buying real estate with little or no money down.

A+
WRITTEN BY WADE B. COOK

A collection of wisdom, thoughts, and principles of success, this book can help you make millions–even billions–of dollars and live an A+ life. As you will see, Wade Cook consistently tries to live his life "in the second mile," to do more than asked, to be above normal. If you want to live a successful life, you need great role models to follow. For years, Wade Cook's life has been a quest to find the successful characteristics of his role models and implement them in his own life. In *A+*, Wade will encourage you to find and incorporate the most successful principles and characteristics of success in your life, too. Don't spend another day living less than an A+ life!

BLUEPRINTS FOR SUCCESS, VOLUME 1
CONTRIBUTORS: WADE COOK, DEBBIE LOSSE, JOEL BLACK, DAN WAGNER, TIM SEMINGSON, RICH SIMMONS, GREGORY WITT, J.J. CHILDERS, KEVEN HART, DAVE WAGNER AND STEVE WIRRICK.

This is a compilation of chapters on building your wealth through your business and making your business function successfully. The chapters cover: education and information gathering, choosing the best business for you from all the different types of business, and a variety of other skills necessary for becoming successful. Your business can't afford to miss out on these powerful insights!

BRILLIANT DEDUCTIONS
WRITTEN BY WADE B. COOK

Do you want to make the most of the money you earn? Do you want to have solid tax havens and ways to reduce the taxes you pay? Learn how to get rich in spite of the updated tax laws. See new tax credits, year-end maneuvers, and methods for transferring and controlling your entities. Learn to structure yourself and your family for tax savings and liability protection.

BUSINESS BUY THE BIBLE
WRITTEN BY WADE B. COOK

Inspired by the Creator, the Bible truly is the authority for running the business of life. Throughout this book, you are provided with practical advice that helps you apply God's word to your life. You'll learn how you can apply God's word to saving, spending and investing, and how you can control debt instead of being controlled by it. You'll also learn how to use God's principles in your daily business activities and prosper.

DON'T SET GOALS (THE OLD WAY)
WRITTEN BY WADE B. COOK

This book will teach you to be a goal-getter, not just a goal-setter. You'll learn that achieving goals is the result of prioritizing and acting. *Don't Set Goals (The Old Way)* shows you how taking action and "paying the price" is more important than simply making the decision to do something. Don't just set goals. Go out and get your goals! Go where you want to go!

HOW TO PICK UP FORECLOSURES
WRITTEN BY WADE B. COOK

Do you want to become an expert money-maker in real estate? This book will show you how to buy real estate at 60¢ on the dollar or less. You'll learn to find the house before the auction and purchase it with no bank financing – the easy way to millions in real estate. The market for foreclosures in a tremendous place to learn and prosper. *How To Pick Up Foreclosures* takes Wade's methods from *Real Estate Money Machine* and supercharges them by applying the fantastic principles to already-discounted properties.

INCORPORATION HANDBOOK
WRITTEN BY WADE B. COOK

Incorporation made easy! This handbook tells you who, why, and, most importantly, how to incorporate. Included are samples of the forms you will use when you incorporate, as well as a step-by-step guide from the experts.

MAKING A LIVING IN THE STOCK MARKET
WRITTEN BY BOB ELDRIDGE

In simplistic, easy to understand terms and presentation, Bob Eldridge shows you how to change your job and your life by *Making a Living in the Stock Market.* This powerful book is full of real life examples of profitable trades. Pages full of charts, diagrams, and tables help the reader understand how these strategies are implemented. If you have little or no money at the end of each paycheck, and have forgotten your dreams in days gone past, this book is for you. You can learn how to make money with cash generating strategies including: channeling stock prices, covered calls, selling naked puts and calls, call (debit) spread, and stock splits.

MILLION HEIRS
WRITTEN BY JOHN V. CHILDERS, JR.

In his reader-friendly style, attorney John V. Childers, Jr. explains how you can prepare your loved ones for when you pass away. He explains many details you need to take care of right away, before a death occurs, as well as strategies for your heirs to utilize. Don't leave your loved ones unprepared – get *Million Heirs*.

ON TRACK INVESTING
WRITTEN BY DAVID HEBERT

On Track Investing is the instruction book for novice stock market investors or anyone who wants to practice investment strategies without risking actual cash. Combined with your personal game plan, the Simutrade™ System helps you originate good trades, perfect your timing, and check your open trades against your personal criteria. There are Simutrade™ Worksheets and step-by-step guides for ten strategies. *On Track Investing* helps you develop a step by step map of what exactly you're going to do and how you're going to accomplish it.

OWNER FINANCING
WRITTEN BY WADE B. COOK

This is a short but invaluable booklet you can give to sellers who hesitate to sell you their property using the owner financing method. Let this pamphlet convince both you and them. The special report, "Why Sellers Should Take Monthly Payments," is included for free in the back of Wade's book, REal Estate Money Machine!

REAL ESTATE FOR REAL PEOPLE
WRITTEN BY WADE B. COOK

A priceless, comprehensive overview of real estate investing, this book teaches you how to buy the right property for the right price, at the right time. Wade Cook explains all of the strategies you'll need, and gives you twenty reasons why you should start investing in real estate today. Learn how to retire rich with real estate, and have fun doing it.

REAL ESTATE MONEY MACHINE
WRITTEN BY WADE B. COOK

Wade's first best-selling book reveals the secrets of his own system – the system he used to earn his first million. This book teaches you how to make money regardless of the state of the economy. Wade's innovative concepts for investing in real estate not only avoid high interest rates, but avoid banks altogether.

ROLLING STOCKS
WRITTEN BY GREGORY WITT

Rolling Stocks shows you the simplest and most powerful strategy for profiting from the ups and downs of the stock market. You'll learn how to find rolling stocks, get in smoothly at the right price, and time your exit. You will learn to recognize the patterns of rolling stocks and how to make the most money from these strategies. Apply rolling stocks principles to improve your trading options and fortify your portfolio.

THE SECRET MILLIONAIRE: GUIDE TO NEVADA CORPORATIONS
WRITTEN BY JOHN V. CHILDERS, JR.

What does it mean to be a secret millionaire? In this book, attorney John V. Childers, Jr. outlines exactly how you can use some of the secret, extraordinary business tactics used by many of today's super-wealthy to protect your assets from the ravages of lawsuits and other destroyers using Nevada Corporations. You'll understand why the state of Nevada has become the preferred jurisdiction for those desiring to establish corporations and how to utilize Nevada Corporations for your financial benefit.

SLEEPING LIKE A BABY
WRITTEN BY JOHN C. HUDELSON

Perhaps the predominant reason people don't invest in the stock market is fear. *Sleeping Like A Baby* helps to remove the fear from investing and give you the confidence and knowledge to invest, wisely, safely, and profitably. You'll learn how to build a high-quality portfolio, plan for your future and let your investments follow. Begin to invest as early as possible, and use proper asset allocation and diversification to reduce risk.

SUCCESS: AMERICAN STYLE
WRITTEN BY WADE B. COOK

Success: American Style is a celebration of this land we call home. This is a collection of sayings – maxims, speeches, quotations, and such about America. These saying range from success to families, from the quality of life to Biblical scriptures and statements. These scriptures and spiritual thoughts are sprinkled throughout this book and were written with the firm belief that this country was kept for this time in God's purpose. People were led here. People with strength, with a desire for freedom and a willingness to pay any price to serve God and their fellow citizens. Our country was destined for greatness, but it can only remain great if we as a people do good works and do great things.

WADE COOK'S POWER QUOTES, VOLUME 1
WRITTEN BY WADE B. COOK

Wade Cook's Power Quotes, Volume 1 is chock full of exciting quotes that have motivated and inspired Mr. Cook, who continually asks his students, "To whom are you listening?" He knows that if you get your advice and inspiration from successful people, you'll become successful yourself. He compiled *Wade Cook's Power Quotes, Volume 1* to provide you with a millionaire-on-call when you need advice.

WEALTH 101
WRITTEN BY WADE B. COOK

This incredible book presents 101 strategies for wealth creation and protection that you can't afford to miss. Front to back, it is packed full of tips to supercharge your financial health. If you need to generate more cash flow, this book shows you how through several various avenues. If you are already wealthy, this book will show you strategy upon strategy for minimizing your tax liability and increasing your peace of mind through liability protection.

SEMINARS AND WORKSHOPS

WALL STREET WORKSHOP™
PRESENTED BY WADE B. COOK AND TEAM WALLSTREET

Once you learn the Wade Cook way of trading stocks and options, your time will belong to you again. The Wade Cook way is not really that different from the strategies the wealthy have used for years. However, it is vastly different than what your typical stockbroker or financial writer will suggest. They want you to turn your money over to a mutual fund manager, broker, or financial planner on the theory that these people know better than you how to take care of your investments.

We believe that no one will take better care of your money than you. Treating the stock market as a business means keeping control of your money, getting educated and how the market works and how you can make it work for you. It means making your own decisions, choosing your own investments, and putting the focus on selling.

After attending the Wall Street Workshop™ and applying Wade Cook's system of "Study, Practice, Understand, then Do," you'll be well on your way to achieving your financial goals. You, too, like thousands of other Wall Street Workshop™ graduates, could be making more money than you ever imagined in the stock market – money you can reinvest for more cash flow, or pull out of your brokerage account and spend tomorrow. With a job-free income from the stock market, a life of freedom awaits you and your family. Start your cash flow education today!

THE NEXT STEP™
PRESENTED BY WADE B. COOK AND TEAM WALL STREET

Continuing quality education is the key to success, and Stock Market Institute of Learning, Inc.™ is dedicated to making that education available to you at every step of your journey to financial freedom. The Next Step™ covers fourteen topics that will let you multiply your returns and dramatically cut losses while you trade the basic Wall Street Workshop™ strategies, plus advanced strategies including puts, spreads and combos.

The information you obtain from this course will dramatically expand your market and financial horizons, By the time you finish the first half of Day One, you'll be too excited to eat! You will learn how to ride the market all directions, and make money consistently. You will hear how you can limit your risk and harness maximum profits in trade after trade.

BUSINESS ENTITY SKILLS TRAINING (B.E.S.T.™)
PRESENTED BY WADE B. COOK AND TEAM WALLSTREET

This one-day seminar is dedicated to teaching new and experienced traders how to do exactly that. You'll learn how to use legal entities such as Nevada corporations, family limited partnerships, and living trusts. People who are creating wealth through the cash-flow strategies taught in the Wall Street Workshop™ need education on how to protect themselves and their loved ones from the three primary destroyers of financial freedom: lawsuits, income taxes, and death taxes. Scheduled to follow most Wall Street Workshops, B.E.S.T.™ is designed to give an overview of basic business entities and correct entity structuring in an one-day format. Your introduction to the world of business entities awaits – it's the B.E.S.T.™!

EXECUTIVE RETREAT™
PRESENTED BY WADE B. COOK AND TEAM WALLSTREET

Many people would think that owning and operating a corporation in today's business world is a complicated and overwhelming task. We fail to realize that thousands of small corporations in our country are operating successfully. Incorporation is a powerful tool for protecting wealth from frivolous lawsuits and over-taxation.

The Executive Retreat instructors are business entity specialists. This hands-on workshop teaches how to set up, manage, and maintain corporations to maximize efficiency and impact your bottom line. This is a unique opportunity for officers of small corporations to network and share information.

FINANCIAL CLINIC
CREATED BY WADE B. COOK AND PRESENTED BY TEAM WALLSTREET

People from all over are making money – lots of money – in the stock market using the proven strategies taught by Wade Cook. Is trading in the stock market for you?

Please accept our invitation to come hear for yourself about the amazing money-making strategies we teach. Our Financial Clinic is designed to help you understand how you can learn these proven stock market strategies. In two and one-half short hours you will be introduced to some of the eleven proven strategies we teach at the Wall Street Workshop™. Discover for yourself how they work and how you can use them in your life to get the things you want for you and your family. Come to this introductory event and see what we have to offer. Then make the decision yourself!

YOUTH WALL STREET WORKSHOP™
PRESENTED BY TEAM WALLSTREET

Wade Cook has made a personal commitment to empower the youth of today with desire and knowledge to be self-sufficient. Now you, too, can make a personal commitment to your youth by sending them to the Youth Wall Street Workshop and start your own family dynasty in the process!

This workshop demonstrates the power and money-making potential of the stock market strategies of the Wall Street Workshop™. The pace is geared to the students, with extra time devoted to vocabulary, principles, and concepts that may be new to them.

Your children and grandchildren can learn these easy to understand strategies and get that "head start" in life! If you're considering the Wall Street Workshop™ for the first time, take advantage of our free Youth Wall Street Workshop promotion and bring a son, daughter, or grandchild with you (ages thirteen to eighteen, student, living at home). Help make your children financially secure in the future by giving them the helping hand in life we all wish we had received.

POOLSIDE INVESTING WITH LEAPS®
PRESENTED BY DARLENE NELSON

If you have been to the Wall Street Workshop, read *Wall Street Money Machine* or been to Stock Split Secrets you are very aware of how exciting trading in the stock market could be…a life-changing event. The difficulty is that many people find their life so full of every day activities that it can be hard to find the time to make trading work. We all have many things on our schedule every day, important things whether it is a career, a family, or your activities in a church or community. What Darlene has brought together in this two-day boot camp is the ability to make the stock market work among the busiest lifestyles. From having a busy life, Darlene has discovered how even the busiest person can make LEAPS® work to their benefit. Whatever you do, you don't want to miss this class.

SEMPER FINANCIAL™ INVESTORS' CONVENTION

Semper Financial Conventions are for everyone! You don't need a financial degree or thousands of dollars to get started making money in the stock market. Anyone who is interested in a brighter financial future for themselves, their spouse, children, friends, church or business associates can come learn these simple cash-flow techniques and formulas in a powerful three-day multi-seminar format.

You owe it yourself to attend a Semper Financial Investors Educational Convention. Never has there been a more exciting way to continue your education or to inexpensively introduce friends and family to stock market strategies for financial freedom!

STOCK SPLIT SECRETS™
PRESENTED BY DARLENE NELSON

Here is the event our students have been asking for! One full day covering the strategy everyone needs to know more about. This event delves deeply into one of Team Wallstreet's™ favorite strategies – Stock Splits. Learn about the power and benefits of stock splits, the motivations behind them, the five phases of a split, the psychology of trading, knowing your exits, having a plan, company analysis. This one-day event, featuring author and speaker Darlene Nelson, gives you a thorough understanding of the dynamics behind Stock Splits. These techniques create a powerful, profitable and predictable plan for earning money in the market.

WEALTH INSTITUTE™
PRESENTED BY WADE B. COOK AND TEAM WALL STREET

During the three days of the Wealth Institute™, we propose to take you on a journey. The directions will be given in simple, understand-able language. Fair warning, though – if you take this journey with us, you may never be the same. Your view of the world of finance will be broader, and your understanding of that world will be deep-ened and improved.

Our journey will take you into the world of entities step by step, explaining who should incorporate, why, and most importantly, how. You will learn about the many tax and other benefits available to corporations. We will teach you the structure and strategies of trusts, limited partnerships, and pensions to maximize your net wealth and minimize your tax burdens. We will also look at the importance of and methods for creating positive cash flow.

There is simply no other course available anywhere like the Wealth Institute. If you want to harness the awesome power of legal entities for yourself or your business, the Wealth Institute is for you. Typical education is about specialization, focusing on the minute details.

You'll learn about connections and synergies – not just how entities work, but how they work together.

VIDEOCASSETTES

180° CASH FLOW TURNAROUND VIDEO
PRESENTED BY WADE B. COOK

Now you know how to make money in any market – up, down, or sideways; if it's moving, you can profit on it! Now spread that knowledge by sharing the 180° Cash Flow Turnaround Seminar on video with your friends, family and co-workers. If you are tired of trying to explain what you are doing in the market, it takes just 180 minutes to turn their stock market thinking around by watching America's premier stock market educator and best-selling author Wade B. Cook!

BUILD PERPETUAL INCOME (BPI)

The Stock Market Institute of Learning™ is proud to present Build Perpetual Income, the latest in our ever-expanding series of seminar home study courses. In this video, you will learn powerful real estate cash-flow generating techniques, such as: power negotiating strategies, buying and selling mortgages, writing contracts, finding and buying discount properties, and avoiding debt.

DYNAMIC DOLLARS VIDEO
PRESENTED BY WADE B. COOK

A very exciting video presentation (about ninety minutes) featuring Wade B. Cook in action. You learn about the power of formulas – including a presentation about rolling stocks, writing covered calls, low–cost, limited–risk options and stock splits – the five times to get involved and uninvolved. You'll get an introduction to the incredible Wall Street Workshop™. Do not go near the stock market until you watch this video. Share it with your stockbroker. Get your family involved. This professional video is literally worth $10,000, many times over. You'll use this information to change the way you look at every trade.

NEXT STEP VIDEO HOME STUDY COURSE
PRESENTED BY TEAM WALL STREET

The advanced version of the Wall Street Workshop™ – full of Wade Cook's power-packed strategies – this is not a duplicate of the Wall Street Workshop™, but a very important partner. The methods taught in this seminar will supercharge the strategies taught in the Wall Street Workshop™ and teach you even more ways to make money!

In the Next Step, you'll learn how to find the stocks to fit the formulas through technical analysis, fundamentals, home trading tools, and more.

RED LIGHT, GREEN LIGHT
PRESENTED BY WADE B. COOK

This is the ultimate on making timely trades. As CEO of a publicly traded company, Wade Cook discovered a quarterly pattern of stock price behavior that corresponds with corporate news reports. Since most companies file their reports about the same time, many stocks would move accordingly.

If you're playing options, those price movements – or lack thereof – have a dramatic effect on your returns. The Red Light, Green Light course shows you how to recognize and use this information to make more money and avoid losing trades. This "news/no-news" discovery is exhilarating!

SPREAD & BUTTER
PRESENTED BY WADE B. COOK

Spread & Butter™ is Wade Cook's tremendously popular one-day seminar on video. Created in early 1999, this home-study course is a live taping of Wade himself teaching his favorite cash flow spread strategies. You will learn everything from basic bull put and bull call spreads to index spreads and calendar spreads, and how to use each effectively.

WALL STREET WORKSHOP VIDEO SERIES
PRESENTED BY WADE B. COOK

If you can't make it to the Wall Street Workshop™ soon, get a head start with these videos. Ten albums containing eleven hours of intense instruction on rolling stocks, options on stock split companies, writing covered calls, and eight other tested and proven strategies designed to help you increase the value of your investments. By learning, reviewing, and implementing the strategies taught here, you will gain the knowledge and the confidence to take control of your investments, and get your money to work hard for you.

MISCELLANEOUS

EXPLANATIONS™ NEWSLETTER

In the wild and crazy stock market game, *EXPLANATIONS* newsletter will keep you on your toes! Every month you'll receive coaching, instruction, and encouragement with engaging articles designed to bring your trading skills to a higher level. Learn new twists on Wade's strategies basic strategies, find out about beneficial research tools, read reviews on the latest investment products and services, and get detailed answers to your trading questions. With *EXPLANATIONS*, you'll learn to be your own best asset in the stock market game and stay on track to a rapidly growing portfolio! Continue your education as an investor and subscribe today!

EXTREME TRADING ANALYSIS SOFTWARE
PRESENTED BY DAVID R. HEBERT

The ETA program is not only designed as a tutorial for the novice trader; its incredible features and benefits make it an important asset to the advanced trader. Features such as the stock transaction record, when used in conjunction with strategy work sheets, will record each trade. This feature is extremely useful, especially at tax time. The program is interactive with WIN and IQ pager, two more powerful tools, that when combined together enhance your research skills they allow you to make <u>educated</u> trading decisions.

THE SUPPORT PACKAGE

SUPPORT is designed to be a one-year continuing education program with six one-day events focused on enhancing your knowledge in specific areas. One of the keys to successful trading is to find a strategy and system that fits your personality, available time, money resources, and risk tolerance. There's no better way to design and implement a personal system than to study several until you identify the one that clicks with your lifestyle and trading goals.

SUPPORT is designed as continuing education for graduates of the Wall Street Workshop™ and others who are interested in specialized training in specific strategies. Students can purchase SUPPORT classes separately or pay a low package price for the right to attend multiple classes of your choosing. Focus on one or two favorite strategies or instructors, or explore several to find the right style for your personality or goals!

TRAVEL AGENT INFORMATION

The only sensible solution for the frequent traveler. This kit includes all of the information and training you need to be an outside travel agent for a stable company. There are no hassles, no requirements, no forms or restrictions, just all the benefits of traveling for substantially less every time.

WEALTH INFORMATION NETWORK™ (W.I.N.™)

This subscription Internet service provides you with the latest financial formulas and updated entity structuring strategies. New, timely information is entered Monday through Friday, sometimes four to five times a day. Wade Cook and his Team Wall Street staff write for W.I.N.™, giving you updates on their own current stock plays, companies who announced earnings, companies who announced stock splits, and the latest trends in the market.

W.I.N.™ is also divided into categories according to specific strategies and contains archives of all our trades so you can view our history. If you are just getting started in the stock market, this is a great way to follow people who are doubling some of their money every two and a half to four months. If you are experienced already, it's the way to confirm your research with others who are generating wealth through the stock market.

Wealth U™

Wealth U™ combines the most powerful, practical and pragmatic training and tools available from the Stock Market Institute of Learning, Inc.™, a company that produces more than thirty powerful live and home-study courses. Our education can and does change people's lives, but we have discovered that often newer students are unsure what classes they need most in order to gain the skills necessary for creating, building and protecting net worth.

Wealth U™ is the answer: a comprehensive yet flexible program of core courses, services and tools rolled into one cost-effective package. Wealth U™ is based on a two-fold vision of financial freedom. The key to this vision is understanding both how to increase income and assets and how to protect that wealth from the challenges of our economic system. Wealth U™ includes everything you need in order to learn, practice and successfully implement our wealth strategies and reach your dreams!

The first goal is to train our students how to amass enough income-producing assets to comfortably support their chosen lifestyle. Wealth U™ courses look at the complexities of the market from several different angles and provide attendees with strategies to help them make educated and profitable trading decisions. Our market strategies can net substantial gains for the student who is willing to study and apply them. Wealth U™ also includes tools to support our students, from home-study courses for review, to an on-line resource for "watching over the shoulders" of professional traders as they implement our strategies in real trade situations.

Our second goal is to help students understand the vehicles available for protecting their assets and income. With diligent practice and careful planning, trading can become your business. To protect the profits of this new business, Wealth U's business classes help students learn to build a new way of life using legal entities such as Nevada corporations, trusts, limited partnerships and more. Wealth U™ students learn how to protect their assets from frivolous lawsuits and excessive taxation.